COUNSELS for JESUITS
Selected Letters
and Instructions of
Saint Ignatius Loyola

Edited by
Joseph N. Tylenda, S.J.

© 1985 Joseph N. Tylenda, S.J.
All rights reserved. Published 1985
Printed in the United States of America

Design by J. L. Boden

Loyola University Press
3441 North Ashland Avenue
Chicago, Illinois 60657

Library of Congress Cataloging in Publication Data

Ignatius, of Loyola, Saint, 1491-1556.
Counsels for Jesuits.

Includes bibliographical references and index.
1. Ignatius, of Loyola, Saint, 1491-1556—Correspondence.
2. Christian saints—Correspondence. 3. Spiritual life—
Catholic authors. 4. Monastic and religious life.
I. Tylenda, Joseph N. II. Title.
BX4700.L7A4   1985   248.4'820942   85-17368
ISBN 0-8294-0496-1

To the memory of John V. McEvoy, S.J.
and to Thomas P. Gavigan, S.J.
who first taught me the wisdom of
St. Ignatius Loyola

CONTENTS

CONTENTS

Contents

CONTENTS

INTRODUCTION

Much of Saint Ignatius Loyola's spiritual teaching is found in his letters, and these have always been regarded by Jesuits as an important source for their spirituality. Among Ignatius's many letters, those written to his fellow Jesuits have always had a special place, for in these the Jesuit of today not only finds Ignatius's teaching on the spiritual life, but he also meets Ignatius the man, expressing his affection for and interest in those to whom he wrote. None of Ignatius's other writings so ably exhibits the love he bore in his heart for those who chose to walk with him along the path toward Christ than do these letters.

This present collection contains forty letters and instructions written to Jesuits, and the reader will find included the ever-famous letters on perfection, obedience, and experiencing the effects of poverty. In fact, these are more than letters, they are short treatises on these very subjects. Also included are Ignatius's instructions on how to deal with others, written when the early Jesuits were leaving Rome as papal legates for Ireland, or as papal theologians to attend the Council of Trent, or when they were on their way to establish the Society in Germany. There are also personal letters encouraging his correspondents, exhorting them to care for their health and moderate their penances, or to view their illness as a gift from God. There are likewise letters of reproof, and though Ignatius writes as Father General, at the same time, he writes as a father to a son; while he corrects his child, he intimates that this correction flows from his paternal love for him.

These forty letters are not newly translated, but are a selection and a revision of the letters translated by William J. Young, S.J., and published as *Letters of St. Ignatius of Loyola* (Chicago: Loyola University Press, 1959). The revision was made with constant reference to the twelve volumes of Ignatius's letters in the *Monumenta Ignatiana* series of the *Monumenta Historica Societatis Iesu (MHSI)* (Madrid, 1903–11). The introductions and notes were written especially for this edition, and in large measure depend on the introductions that precede Ignatius's letters in the fourth revised edition of *Obras Completas de San Ignacio de Loyola*

(Madrid: Biblioteca de Autores Cristianos, 1982), edited by Ignacio Iparraguirre, S.I., and Candido de Dalmases, S.I.

In this present edition each letter is preceded by a short introduction, identifying the recipient of the letter and indicating or explaining the occasion for the letter. The letters are given in chronological order and cover the years from September 1541, to July 18, 1556, two weeks before Ignatius's death. Toward the end of each introduction, reference is made to where the letter may be found in the volumes of the *Monumenta Ignatiana*.

Solemnity of Mary and the
Giving of the Name Jesus
January 1, 1985

1. TO FATHERS BROËT AND SALMERÓN

On Dealing with   Rome,
Others   early September 1541

In November 1538, Ignatius placed himself and his
companions at the disposal of Pope Paul III and expressed his
and their willingness to be sent wherever the pope needed
them. Within a short time the pontiff called on the Jesuits to
go to Siena, Parma, and India. Now, at the suggestion of the
English cardinal, Reginald Pole, Paul III chose to send
Paschase Broët[1] and Alfonso Salmerón[2] as legates to Ireland to
help stem the spread of King Henry VIII's heretical ideas.
Their task was to visit bishops, reform the monasteries, and
rekindle the faith among the Irish people. They left Rome on
September 10, 1541. Ignatius prepared three instructions for
these Jesuits; the one translated below gives the norms they
are to follow in their apostolate. They are to adapt themselves
to the temperaments of the individuals with whom they deal
and, to win them over, they are instructed to enter the other's
door but to come out their own. This instruction was
prepared in early September 1541, and was written in Spanish
[Ep. 1:179–81].

How to Deal and Converse
with Others in the Lord

In all your dealings be slow to speak and say little, especially with
your equals and those lower in dignity and authority than
yourselves. Be ready to listen for long periods and until each one
has had his say. Answer the questions put to you, come to an end,
and take your leave. If a rejoinder is required, let your reply be as
brief as possible, and take leave promptly and politely.

In dealing with men of position or influence—if you hope to
win their affection for the greater glory of God our Lord—first
consider their temperaments and adapt yourselves to them. If they

1

are of a lively temper, quick, and cheerful in speech, follow their lead while speaking to them of good and holy things, and do not be serious, glum, and reserved. If they are shy and retiring, slow to speak, serious, and weighty in their words, use the same manner with them, because such ways will be pleasing to them. *I became all things to all men* [1 Cor. 9:22].

You must keep in mind that if someone with a lively disposition does not deal with another who is likewise lively, there is very great danger of their failing to come to any agreement, since they happen not to be of the same mind. And therefore, if one knows that he himself is of such a lively disposition, he ought to approach the other, possessing similar traits, well prepared by a close study of himself and determined to be patient and not to get out of sorts with him, especially if he knows him to be in poor health. If he is dealing with one of slower temper, then there is not so much danger of a disagreement arising from words too hastily spoken.

Whenever we wish to win someone over and engage him in the greater service of God our Lord, we should use the same strategy for good that the enemy employs to draw a good soul to evil. The enemy enters through the other's door and comes out his own. He enters with the other, not by opposing his ways but by praising them. He acts familiarly with the soul, suggesting good and holy thoughts which bring peace to the good soul. Then, little by little, he tries to come out his own door, always portraying some error or illusion under the appearance of something good, but which will always be evil. So, we may lead others to good by praising or agreeing with them on a certain good point, leaving aside whatever else may be wrong. Thus after gaining his confidence, we shall meet with better success. In this sense we enter his door with him, but we come out our own.

We should be kind and compassionate with those who are sad or tempted, speak at length with them, and show great joy and cheerfulness, both interior and exterior, to draw them to the opposite of what they feel, for their greater edification and consolation.

In everything you say, especially when you are trying to restore peace and are giving spiritual exhortations, be on your guard and remember that everything you say may or will become public.

In business matters be generous with your time; that is, if you can, do today what you promise to do tomorrow.

On the supposition that you possess such authority, it would be better if Master Francis[3] had charge of the finances. You will be better able to accept or decline requests coming from others if none of the three of you touch any money, but rather send it by another to the person to whom it is due. In fact, it would be better for the person seeking the dispensation to give the fee directly to the person to whom it is owed, and get a receipt indicating that the dispensation was granted. Or, if any other way be more convenient, use it, but see to it that each of the three of you can say that he has not touched any money connected with the mission.

2. TO FATHER GIOVANNI BATTISTA VIOLA

On Obedience   Rome, August 1542

Father Viola[4] was among the first Italians to enter the Society. In 1541 Ignatius sent him to Paris for further studies and to be, at the same time, superior of the young Jesuits attending the university. Before Viola left for Paris on October 14, 1541, Ignatius advised him that, since he would be arriving several months after the school year had begun, it would be good for him to spend his first months brushing up on his Latin and studying the Súmulas (the Summulae logicales of Peter of Spain), to be ready to begin his studies the following year. But Viola, hoping that he could save time and thinking that he was sufficiently prepared, immediately began his work at the university. In the end he found that it was too much for him and that he had wasted his time. During the summer of 1542 he wrote to Ignatius; although his letter is not extant, its contents are clear from Ignatius's response. Viola complained that he had wasted eight months with his teacher and now he was asking Ignatius what he should do. Ignatius approaches the question from the viewpoint of blind obedience. Viola lost time because he had not followed the instructions he received before leaving Rome. The letter's date is probably August 1542, and was written in Spanish [Ep. 1:228–29].

Jhus

May the sovereign grace and love of Christ our Lord be our never-failing help and support.

I received your letter but I fail to understand it. In two different places you speak of obedience. In the first you say that you are ready to obey me, and in the second you say: "Because I would rather die than fail in obedience, I submit to the judgment of your reverence." Now, it seems to me that obedience seeks to be blind, and is blind in two ways: in the first it belongs to the inferior to submit his understanding, when there is no question of sin, and to do what is commanded of him; in the second it is also the inferior's duty, once the superior commands or has commanded something, to represent to the superior whatever considerations or disadvantages may occur to him, and to do so humbly and simply, without any attempt to draw the superior to either side, so that afterwards he can follow, with peace of mind, the way pointed out to him or commanded.

Now, applying this to your obedience, I am unable to understand it. For after you have given me many good arguments to persuade me to approve another teacher, you tell me elsewhere in your letter: "It has seemed good to me to write your reverence to ask you kindly to let me know whether I should change teachers or go on wasting my time."

You yourself can judge whether you are seeking to obey, or whether you are submitting your judgment to whatever decision I make. If you so abound in judgment of your own and are convinced that you are wasting your time, where is the submission of your judgment? Indeed, do you think that I am going to tell you to waste

4

your time? May God our Lord never let me harm anyone when I cannot help him!

In another place you say: "I am truly sorry to have wasted these last eight months under this teacher but, nevertheless, if you think I should go on wasting it, I will continue with him." I recall that I told you, when you left here, that by the time you reached Paris the course in the *Súmulas* would have been in progress for two or three months, and that you should start by studying Latin for four or five months and then take the elements of the *Súmulas* for three or four months so that with this preparation you could begin the regular course the following year. But following your own ideas rather than mine, you saw fit to enter a course already two or three months in session. Judge for yourself who is the cause of your wasting time!

I close asking our Lord in His infinite goodness to give us the fullness of His perfect grace, so that we may know His most holy will and perfectly fulfill it.

From Rome.

3. TO FATHER PIERRE FAVRE

On Writing Letters Rome, December 10, 1542

Pierre Favre[5] had been Ignatius's first companion in Paris. At the time of this letter Favre was, by order of Pope Paul III, at the court of Emperor Charles V in Germany. Ignatius here explains to Favre the care with which Jesuits should write their letters, and he asks him to write a principal letter every two weeks, which can be shown to members of the Society and to others as well, especially those interested in the works of the Society. They should devote this principal letter to a description of their spiritual activities, and are to leave the more mundane, but interesting, news items for additional enclosures. Ignatius found that not only Favre was deficient in this matter, but so was every other Jesuit; thus he informs Favre that he was sending copies of the letter to others as well. Ignatius wrote this letter in Spanish [Ep. 1:236–38].

Jhs

I recall having frequently told you and, when you were away, having often written, that each member of the Society should, when they write to us here, write out a principal letter which can be shown to others; that is, to anyone at all. We dare not show some letters to friendly eyes who wish to see them, because of their lack of order and the irrelevant items they contain. Now, these friends are aware that we have letters from this one and that one, and they feel offended if we refuse to let them see these letters; thus we cause more disedification than edification. Quite recently it happened that I was put to considerable inconvenience. I had to show some letters from two of Ours to two cardinals who were personally interested in the contents of those letters. But because the letters also contained matters that were irrelevant to their business and were set down without order, it was hard to withhold what did not concern them.

I must repeat what I have said before, so that we may all understand one another on each and every point. I beg of you, therefore, by the love and reverence of God our Lord, to see to it that your letter writing be directed to the greater service of His Divine Goodness and the greater advantage of our neighbor. In the principal letter put down what each one is doing regarding preaching, hearing confessions, giving the Exercises, and other spiritual activities, as God makes use of each for the greater edification of our hearers and readers. If the soil you are working be unproductive and there be little to write about, put down briefly something about health, your dealings with others, or such matters. Do not include irrelevant details but leave them for separate sheets in which you can write about letters received and the spiritual consolation they have given you, items of news, especially about the sick, business matters, and even some words by way of exhortation.

I will set down what my own practice is, and I hope in our Lord will continue to be, in writing to members of the Society. It helps keep me from making mistakes. I write the principal letter once, putting down what will be edifying, and then I reread and correct it, keeping in mind that everyone is going to read it. Then I write it out a second time, or have someone else do it, for whatever appears in writing needs closer scrutiny than what is merely spoken; the written word remains as a perpetual witness which cannot be amended or explained away as is easily done with speech. Even with all this I am sure that I make mistakes and I fear I will do so in the future. Other details which would be irrelevant in the principal letter, or which might not be edifying, I leave for the separate sheets. In these sheets one may write hurriedly out of the abundance of the heart, with or without a predetermined order. But this should not be true of the principal letter, which should always show signs of care, so that it can be passed about to give edification.

Everyone seems to have failed in this regard, and so a copy of this letter is being sent to all. I beg and beseech you in our Lord to write out the main or principal letter as I have here indicated and then, after looking it over, rewrite it; that is, it should be written twice, as I do with mine. In this way I am convinced that the letters will show greater order and clarity. In the future, if I notice that this is not being done for the greater union, charity, and edification of all, I shall be obliged to write you and command you under obedience to reread, correct, and rewrite every principal letter you send me. I do not want to have to answer to God for any negligence of my own in this matter, and I shall be satisfied with having done all that I could, though I should much prefer that you give me no occasion for so writing to you.

I exhort you, then, as I am bound to do for the greater glory of God our Lord, and I beg of you by His love and reverence to improve your writing and to conceive some appreciation for it, as well as a desire to edify your brethren and your neighbor by your letters. Be assured that the time you spend at it—it can be put down to my account—will be spent in our Lord. It costs me an effort to write a principal letter twice, to give it some appearance of order, to say nothing of the many additional sheets. Even this letter I have twice written with my own hand; how much more, then, should each member of the Society do likewise? You have to write to one person only, but I have to write to everyone. I can truthfully say that the other night we counted the letters which we were sending to various places and found that there were two hundred and fifty. If some of you in the Society are busy, I am convinced that I am no less busy than any of you, and with poorer health than you.

Up to the present I cannot praise a single one of you in this matter, yet I do not wish to find fault. If the copies of the letters from others which I send you seem to be arranged in some order and contain little superfluous, it is because, at no little loss of time, I have selected what is edifying, rearranging the very words they use, and cutting out those that are irrelevant, to give all of you some pleasure in our Lord and edification for those who hear them for the first time. So, again I beg of you, by your love and reverence for the Divine Majesty, put your heart in this matter and get to work with all diligence; it will greatly contribute toward the spiritual progress and consolation of souls. Every two weeks write a principal letter, revised, and corrected, which, all told, will be really the work of two letters. In the sheets, where you have to write only to the individual who is to use them, you may be as long as you like. With God's help I will write all of you once a month without fail, but briefly; and more at length every three months, when I will send all the news and copies of all the letters I receive from Ours. Let us all, therefore, for the love of God our Lord, help one another. And do me the favor of bearing with me, and in some way lighten the heavy burden you have placed on my shoulders, to say nothing of other tasks that await me here: I mean works of piety and other spiritually profitable works. If I could do the work of ten, or if we were all together here in Rome, we would have more than we could handle. In case your memory fails, as mine does often enough, keep this letter or a digest of it before you when you write your principal letters.

From Rome, December 10, 1542.

4. TO THE FATHERS ATTENDING THE COUNCIL OF TRENT

On Dealing with Others   Rome, early 1546

*The Council of Trent opened on December 13, 1545. Pope
Paul III had asked Ignatius for three Jesuits to serve as
theologians to the three legates presiding over the council; in
response to this request, Ignatius appointed Diego Laínez,[6]
Alfonso Salmerón,[7] and Pierre Favre.[8] Laínez and Salmerón
arrived in Trent on May 18, 1546; Claude Jay[9] had already
been there since the previous December representing
Cardinal Truchsess of Augsburg. Favre, however, was never
to arrive. He was in Spain preparing the way for future houses
of the Society when he received word of his appointment, but
he wanted to visit Ignatius in Rome before going to Trent.
Thus he sailed from Barcelona, landed at Genoa, and made his
way to Rome, arriving there on July 17, 1546. His health had
been greatly weakened by the frequent bouts of fever he had
suffered over the past years, and before he had a chance to
leave Rome for Trent the fever returned and he died on
August 1. At Trent Laínez and Salmerón were assigned the
task of making abstracts from Protestant books and
extracting propositions for discussion in the council; both
Jesuits frequently spoke before the assembled fathers. Before
these Jesuits had left Rome in early 1546, Ignatius wrote an
instruction for their benefit and in it he offers his advice on
how to deal with others at the council, encourages them to
initiate an apostolate among the people of the city, and
suggests some self-helps. Ignatius did not view the position of
peritus as a full-time job, for besides their regular work at the
council they were to preach, hear confessions, visit the sick
and poor, teach catechism to children, and give the Exercises
to those ready for them. This instruction was written
sometime in early 1546 and is in Spanish [Ep. 1:386–89].*

Instruction for the Sojourn at Trent

Ihs

Dealing with Others

1. Since associating and dealing with many people for the salvation and spiritual progress of souls can be very profitable with God's help so, on the other hand, if we are not on our guard and helped by God's grace, such association can be the occasion of great loss to ourselves and sometimes to everyone concerned. In keeping with our profession we cannot withdraw from such association and, therefore, the more prepared we are to proceed according to a common plan, the more likely we are to succeed in our Lord. In the following notes, which may be modified or amplified according to need, we may be able to offer some assistance.

2. Be slow to speak. Be considerate and kind, especially when it comes to deciding on matters under discussion, or about to be discussed in the council.

3. Be slow to speak, and only after having first listened quietly, so that you may understand the meaning, leanings, and wishes of those who do speak. Thus you will better know when to speak and when to be silent.

4. When these or other matters are under discussion, I should consider the reasons on both sides without showing any attachment to my own opinion, and try to avoid bringing dissatisfaction to anyone.

5. I should not cite anyone as supporting my opinion, especially if they are persons of importance, unless this has been thoroughly arranged beforehand. And I would deal with everyone on an equal basis, never taking sides with anyone.

6. If the matters being discussed are of such a nature that you cannot or ought not to be silent, then give your opinion with the greatest possible humility and sincerity, and always end with the words *salvo meliori iudicio*—with due respect for a better opinion.

7. Finally, if some point of human or divine science is under discussion and I have something to say, it will be of great help to forget about my own leisure or lack of time—that is, my own convenience. I should rather accommodate myself to the convenience

of him with whom I am to deal, so that I may influence him to God's greater glory.

Helping Souls

1. While at Trent Ours should try to live together in some respectable district. And what they should especially seek to accomplish for God's greater glory is to preach, hear confessions, lecture, instruct children, give good example, visit the poor in the hospitals, and exhort the neighbor according to the talents each is conscious of possessing, so as to move as many as possible to prayer and devotion. Pray and lead others to pray particularly to God our Lord, beseeching His Divine Majesty to deign to send forth His Holy Spirit on all who take part in the discussions of that august gathering, so that the Holy Spirit may descend in greater abundance with His grace and gifts upon the council.

2. In your sermons do not touch on subjects on which Catholics and Protestants are at variance, but simply exhort your audience to virtue and to devotions approved by the Church. Awaken in souls a thorough knowledge of themselves and a love of their Creator and Lord. Speak frequently of the council and always end your sermons, as we have said, with a prayer for the council.

3. In lecturing follow the same rules as you do in preaching, and try to enkindle in souls a love of their Creator and Lord, explaining the meaning of the passage read, and have your hearers pray as has been indicated.

4. When you hear confessions remember to tell your penitents the same that you have said in public. Let the penance consist of prayers for the council.

5. In giving the Exercises and in other conversations, remember that you are equivalently speaking in public. Recall that, in general, only the exercises of the first week should be given to everyone, unless you are dealing with very special persons who are prepared to arrange their lives according to the manner of the elections. Such persons should not be allowed to make any vows, either during the Exercises or at their end; nor should they bind themselves in any other way, especially at the beginning. Later on, if time allows, they might do so, but always with moderation, and

only if the Exercises are given them in their entirety. Prayers for the council should also be said.

6. You should teach boys at some appropriate time, according to an arrangement that is suitable and which may vary in different places. Begin with the basic rudiments and explain them in keeping with the needs of your audience. When you end your instruction recite some prayers for the council.

7. Visit the hospitals at some convenient hour during the day, always taking your health into consideration. Hear the confessions of the poor and console them, and even take them some little gift if you can. Have them pray, as I have suggested when speaking of hearing confessions. If you are at least three in number, each one should take his turn visiting the poor, a day at a time, twice a week.

8. Exhort those with whom you come into contact to frequent confession, Communion, or the celebration of Mass. Have them make the Exercises and perform other works of piety; also encourage them to pray for the council.

9. Here also, as in determining the matters to be discussed, it will be better to be slow to speak and to speak little, as I have said. But on the other hand, if you wish to urge souls to make progress in the spiritual life, it will be better to speak at length, with order, and with kindness and love.

Some Self-Helps

Spend an hour at night when each of you can share with the others what you have done that day and discuss your plans for the following day.

We should agree on past and future matters by vote, or in some other way.

On one night, let one of you ask the others to correct him in what he may have done amiss, and he who is corrected should make no answer unless he is asked to explain the matter about which he has been corrected. On another night, another will do the same. And thus each one in turn, so that all can be helped unto greater charity and to greater influence in all things.

Make your resolutions in the morning and twice during the day make the examen.

This order should begin within five days of your arrival at Trent. Amen.

5. TO THE FATHERS AND BROTHERS STUDYING AT COIMBRA

On Perfection   Rome, May 7, 1547

Simão Rodrigues[10] introduced the Society into Portugal in 1540 and founded the college at Coimbra in 1542. At the time of this letter there were eighty scholastics studying at the college, and from various sources, notably from Rodrigues, who was provincial, and from Martín de Santa Cruz,[11] who was rector of the community, Ignatius learned of certain "holy follies" practiced by these young Jesuits. Their excessive fervor led them to discipline themselves in the city streets, preach half-clothed, and raise penitential cries in the middle of the night. These "holy follies" seem to have had the provincial's approval. Rodrigues wrote to Ignatius at the beginning of 1547,[12] telling him about the outstanding fervor among the scholastics and noted that there was division in the community regarding public manifestations of that fervor, and so he asked Ignatius to write them a letter on this very matter. In his letter Ignatius tells the scholastics of the need to restrain their fervor. Excess can easily lead to pride and vanity, loss of health, as well as other inconveniences, and thus Ignatius instructs them to put an end to their practices. The letter has three parts: (1) Ignatius first praises the fervor in the young Jesuits and encourages them to continue to be fervent in their vocation; (2) then he tells them of the need to restrain that fervor, lists the harm that can arise from excessive fervor, and suggests that if they want to arrive at discretion they must practice obedience; (3) finally, he enumerates the ways that the young scholastics may exercise zeal during their years of study, for example, offering their studies to God, growing in virtue, and giving good example. The headings within the letter have been added for the sake of clarity; the original letter was written in Spanish [Ep. 1:495–510].

May the grace and everlasting love of Christ our Lord be ever our protection and help. Amen.

Introduction

Master Simão's letter and that of Santa Cruz bring me continued news about you, and God, from whom all good things come, knows what comfort and joy it gives me to see that He so helps you, not only in your studies but in your pursuit of virtue as well. Indeed, the fragrance of these virtues has carried to very distant lands, to the encouragement and edification of many. And if every Christian should rejoice because of the common obligation we all have of seeking God's honor and the welfare of His image, which has been redeemed by the blood and death of Jesus Christ, I have a special reason for rejoicing in our Lord, seeing that I have a distinct obligation of keeping you in my heart with a special affection. May our Creator and Redeemer be ever blessed and praised for all, since it is from His liberality that every blessing and grace flows, and may it please Him every day to open more and more the fountain of His mercy to increase and advance what He has already begun in your souls. I have no doubt concerning that Supreme Goodness, who is so eager to share His blessings, or of that everlasting love which makes Him more eager to bestow perfection on us than we are to receive it. If this were not so, our Lord Jesus Christ would never encourage us to hope for what we can have only from His generous hand. For He tells us: *Be you therefore perfect, as also your heavenly Father is perfect* [Matt. 5:48]. Thus it is certain that for His part He is ready to bestow it, on condition that we have a vessel of humility and desire to receive His graces, and that He sees that we use well the gifts we have received and cooperate diligently and earnestly with His grace.

Part I
Incentives toward Advancement

The Excellence of a Vocation

On this point I will not fail to put the spurs even to those of you who are running so willingly. For I can tell you that you must be constant, both in your studies and in the practice of virtue, if you are to fulfill the expectations which so many entertain of you. Some persons, in both the kingdom of Portugal and in many other countries, considering the helps and advantages of every kind, both interior and exterior, that God gives you, rightly hope for more than ordinary results from you.

No commonplace achievement will satisfy the great obligations you have of excelling. If you consider the nature of your vocation, you will see that what would be thought outstanding in others would not be so in you. For not only has God *called you out of darkness into His marvelous light* [1 Pet. 2:9], and *translated you into the kingdom of His beloved Son* [Col. 1:13], as He has done with the rest of the faithful, but because you have better preserved purity and are more united in His service in the love of spiritual things, He thought it good to withdraw you from the perilous sea of this world to preserve your consciences from the dangers of the storms which the gusts of passion are wont to raise—the desire now of possessions, now of honors, now of pleasures—and, on the other hand, from the fear of losing all such things. Another reason, over and above this, is that if these earthly concerns have no place in your thoughts or affections, you will be preserved from distraction and dissipation, so that you will be able to direct your thoughts and affections and employ them in attaining the end for which God created you: that is, His own honor and glory, your own salvation, and the help of your neighbor.

It is true that all orders in the Church are directed to this end. And yet God has called you to this one, in which His glory and the salvation of the neighbor are set before you, not as a general end but one toward which your whole life and its various activities must be directed as a continuous sacrifice. This requires a cooperation from you that should not stop with example and earnest prayer, but includes all the exterior means which His Divine Providence has provided for the mutual help we should give one another. From this you can understand how noble and royal is the manner of life you have chosen. For not merely among men, but not even among the angels, is there a nobler work than glorifying the Creator and leading His creatures to Him, as far as their capacities permit.

The Advantages of Fervor

Therefore, give serious thought to your vocation so that you can give much thanks to God for so great a favor and ask Him for the special help needed to correspond to it with courage and diligence. Both of these you must have in large measure if you are to attain the end you have in view. Sloth, tepidity, weariness in study and in the other exercises which you have undertaken for the love of our Lord you must recognize as the sworn enemies of your vocation.

For his encouragement each one should keep before his eyes, not those who he thinks will accomplish less, but rather those who are active and energetic. Never permit the children of this world to show greater care and interest in the things of time than you show for those of eternity. It should bring a blush to your cheek to see them run to death more enthusiastically than you to life. Hold yourselves as worth little if a courtier serves with greater dedication to gain the favor of an earthly prince than you do for the favor of the King of Heaven, or if a soldier battles with greater courage for the glory of victory and hope of spoils, than you fight for victory and triumph over the world, the devil, and yourselves, all for a heavenly kingdom and eternal glory.

For the love of God, therefore, be neither careless nor tepid. For if tautness snaps the bow, slackness snaps the soul; while on the contrary, according to Solomon, *the soul of them that work shall be richly supplied* [Prov. 13:4]. Try to maintain a holy and discreet fervor in your work and in the pursuit of learning as well as virtue. With both alike, one energetic act is worth a thousand that are listless, and what a lazy man cannot accomplish in many years an energetic man can usually quickly achieve.

In the matter of learning, the difference between the earnest and the careless student stands out clearly. The same holds true in the mastering of passion and the weaknesses to which our nature is subject, as in the acquiring of virtue. It is certain that, because the negligent do not struggle against self, they never achieve peace of soul or do so tardily, and never possess any virtue in its fullness, while the energetic and industrious make notable advances on both fronts.

Experience proves that in this life peace and satisfaction are had, not by the listless but by those who are fervent in God's service. And rightly so. For in their effort to overcome themselves

16

and to rid themselves of self-love, they rid themselves of the roots of all passion and unrest. And by acquiring habits of virtue, they naturally succeed in acting with ease and cheerfulness in accordance with these same virtues.

By this means they dispose themselves to receive the holy consolations of God our faithful consoler, for *to him who conquers I will give the hidden manna* [Rev. 2:17]. On the other hand, tepidity is the cause of a lifetime of uneasiness, for we never uproot its cause, self-love, nor do we ever deserve God's help. Therefore you should rouse yourselves to work earnestly at your praiseworthy tasks, since even in this life you will perceive the advantages of holy fervor, not only in the growth of perfection in your souls but even in the peace of mind it grants you in this present life.

But if you look to the eternal reward, as often you should, Saint Paul will easily convince you that *the sufferings of this time are not worthy to be compared with the glory to come that shall be revealed in us* [Rom. 8:18], because *this slight momentary affliction is preparing for us an eternal measure of glory beyond all comparison* [2 Cor. 4:17].

If this is true of every Christian who serves and honors God, you can understand what your crown will be if you correspond with our Institute, which is not only to serve God for your own sakes but to draw many others to His honor and service. Of them Holy Scripture says that *they that instruct many to justice shall shine as stars for all eternity* [Dan. 12:3]. And this is to be understood of those who engage in the discharge of their duty, not only later in the exercise of arms but even before that, while they are getting themselves ready. If this were not so, we certainly could not apply to works that are in themselves good the words of Jeremiah, *Cursed is he that does the work of the Lord carelessly* [Jer. 48:10], and of Saint Paul, *Do you not know that in a race all indeed run, but only one receives the prize?* [1 Cor. 9:24], and *for he is not crowned unless he strives according to the rules* [2 Tim. 2:5], and that means a good worker.

God's Manifold Gifts

But more than anything else I should wish to awaken in you the pure love of Jesus Christ, the desire for His honor and for the salvation of souls whom He has redeemed. For you are His soldiers

17

in this Society with a special title and a special wage. I say special because there are many general reasons which likewise oblige you to work for His honor and service. His wage is everything you are and have in the natural order, for He bestows and preserves your being and life, and all the perfections of body and soul, as well as eternal blessings. His wage is also the spiritual gifts of His grace with which He has so generously and lovingly bestowed on you and continues to offer even when you oppose Him and rebel against Him. His wage is also those incomparable blessings of His glory which, without any advantage to Himself, He has promised to you and holds in readiness for you, actually sharing with you all the treasures of His happiness so that you may, by a remarkable participation in His divine perfection, be what He is by essence and nature. Finally, His wage is the whole universe and everything material and spiritual contained in it. For He has placed under our ministry not only all that is under heaven, but even the whole of His sublime court, without exempting any of the heavenly hierarchy: *Are they not all ministering spirits, sent to minister for them who shall receive the inheritance of salvation?* [Heb. 1:14].

As though this wage were not enough, He has made Himself our wage, becoming a brother in our own flesh, as the price of our salvation on the cross, and in the Eucharist to be with us as support and company. Oh, what an unworthy soldier he would be whom such a wage would not induce to labor for the honor of such a prince. We know indeed that, to oblige us to desire and labor for this glory, His Majesty has bestowed on us these inestimable and priceless favors, in a sense stripping Himself of His own possessions to give us a share in them; taking on Himself our miseries to deliver us from them; wishing to be sold as our redemption; to be dishonored to glorify us; to be poor to enrich us; accepting a disgraceful and painful death to give us a blessed and immortal life. How extremely ungrateful and hardhearted is he who after all this does not recognize his obligation to serve our Lord Jesus Christ diligently and to seek His honor.

The Wretched State of Many Souls and of the World

If, therefore, you recognize this obligation, and wish to employ yourselves in promoting God's honor, the times you are living in indeed require that you make your desire known by works. Can you find a place where the Divine Majesty is in honor today, or where His infinite greatness is worshiped, where His wisdom and infinite goodness are known, or His most holy will obeyed? Behold rather, with deep grief, how His holy name is everywhere ignored, despised, blasphemed. The teaching of Jesus Christ is cast off, His example forgotten, and the price of His blood lost, in a sense, as far as we are concerned, because so few profit by it. Behold also your neighbors, images of the most holy Trinity and capable of enjoying the glory of Him whom all the world serves, members of Christ, redeemed by so much pain, opprobrium, and blood. Behold, I say, the miseries that surround them, the darkness of ignorance that envelops them, and the whirlwind of desires, empty fears, and other passions that torment them, set upon by so many visible and invisible enemies, in danger of losing, I do not say their wealth or temporal life, but an eternal kingdom and its happiness by falling into the insufferable misfortune of everlasting fire.

To sum up briefly, if you were carefully to examine the great obligation you have of seeking the honor of Jesus Christ and the salvation of your neighbor, you would see how fitting it is for you to get ready by diligently striving to make yourselves fit instruments of God's grace, especially since in these days there are so few real laborers who do not seek the things that are their own, but the things that are Jesus Christ's. And the more others fall short, the more you ought to endeavor to make up for them, since God bestows so special a grace on you and one so proper to your vocation.

Part II
The Need to Beware of Excessive Fervor

Harm Coming from Excessive Fervor

What I have said so far to awaken the drowsy and spur on the loiterers on the way, should not be taken as a justification for going to the other extreme of fervor. Spiritual infirmities such as tepidity are caused, not only by chills but also by fevers, that is, by excessive zeal. Saint Paul says, *let your service be a reasonable service* [Rom. 12:1], because he knew the truth of the words of the Psalmist, *the king in his might loves justice* [99:4], that is, discretion; and what was prefigured in Leviticus, *whatsoever sacrifice you offer, you shall season it with salt* [2:13]. In the same vein does Saint Bernard speak: the enemy has no more successful ruse for depriving the heart of real charity than to get her to act rashly and not in keeping with spiritual reasonableness.[13] "Nothing in excess," said the philosopher.[14] And this principle should be our guide even in a matter pertaining to justice itself, as we read in Ecclesiastes, *be not over just* [7:16]. If one fails to observe this moderation, he will find that good is turned into evil and virtue into vice. He will also learn that many inconveniences follow which are quite contrary to the purpose of the one who so acts.

The first is that God is not really served in the long run, as the horse worn out in the first days does not as a rule finish the journey, and thus it happens that someone must be found to care for it.

Second, gains that are made through such excessive eagerness do not usually endure, as Scripture says, *wealth gathered in haste will dwindle* [Prov. 13:11]. Not only dwindle, but it may be the cause of a fall: *and he that is hasty with his feet shall stumble* [Prov. 19:2]; and if he stumbles, the further he falls, the greater the danger, for he will not stop until he has reached the bottom of the ladder.

Third, there is the danger of being careless in overloading the vessel. There is danger, of course, in sailing it empty, as it can then be tossed about on the waves of temptation; but there is also danger of so overloading it that it sinks.

Fourth, it can happen that, in crucifying the old man, the new man is also crucified and thus made unable through weakness to practice virtue. Saint Bernard tells us that because of this excess we lose four things: "The body loses the effect of the good work, the soul its devotion, our neighbor good example, and God His honor."[15] From this we infer that whosoever thus mistreats the living temple of God is guilty of sacrilege. Saint Bernard says that the neighbor is deprived of good example, because the fall of one and the ensuing scandal are a source of scandal to others; and he calls them, in cause at least, disturbers of unity and enemies of peace. The example of such a fall frightens many and makes them tepid in their spiritual progress. In the fallen there is danger of pride and vainglory, since they prefer their own judgment to the judgment of everyone else, usurping what is not their own by setting themselves up as judges in their own cause when the rightful judge is their superior.

Besides these, there are also other disadvantages, such as overloading themselves with weapons which they cannot use, like David with the armor of Saul [1 Sam. 17:38–39]. They apply spurs to a spirited horse rather than the rein. Therefore there is need of discretion on this point to keep the practice of virtue between both extremes. Saint Bernard gives this advice: "Good will is not always to be trusted, but it must be bridled, regulated, especially in beginners,"[16] if one wishes to benefit others without any disadvantage to himself, for *he that is evil to himself, to whom will he be good?* [Sir. 14:5].

Obedience is the Infallible Means for Gaining Discretion

If discretion seems to you to be something very rare and hard to come by, make up for it with obedience, whose counsel is certain. Hear what Saint Bernard says of those who wish to follow their own opinion: "Whatever is done without the approval or against the wishes of the spiritual father should be set down as vainglory, and not as something worthy of reward."[17] We should remember, as it is said in Holy Scripture, that *it is like the sin of witchcraft to rebel, and like the crime of idolatry to refuse to obey* [1 Sam. 15:23]. Thus if you wish to hold the middle way between the extremes of tepidity and excessive fervor, discuss your affairs with the superior and keep within the limits set down by obedience. If you have a great desire for mortification, use it rather in breaking your wills and bringing your judgments under the yoke of obedience rather than in weakening your bodies and afflicting them beyond due measure, especially during the years of your studies.

Part III
Ways of Exercising Zeal During Years of Study

Offer Your Studies to God

I should not wish you to think from what I have here written that I do not approve of what I have learned of some of your mortifications. I know that these and other holy follies have been profitably used by the saints and that they are useful to obtain self-mastery and bring down richer graces upon us, especially in the beginning. But for one who has acquired some mastery over his self-love, I hold that what I have written about bringing oneself to the golden mean of discretion is the better thing, provided one does not withdraw from obedience. It is this obedience that I recommend very earnestly to you, joined with that virtue which is a compendium of all the others and which Jesus Christ so earnestly recommends when He calls it His special commandment: *This is my commandment, that you love one another* [John 15:12]. And I wish that you preserve this union and lasting love, not only among yourselves, but that you extend it to everyone, and endeavor to enkindle in your souls the lively desire for the salvation of your neighbor, gauging the value of each soul from the price our Lord paid by His life's blood. This you do on the one hand by acquiring learning and on the other by increasing fraternal charity, making yourselves perfect instruments of God's grace and collaborators in the sublime work of leading God's creatures back to Him as to their last end.

Do not think that in this period of time given to your studies you are of no use to your neighbor, for, besides the profit to yourself which well-ordered charity requires—*Have pity on your own soul, pleasing God* [Vulgate Sir. 30:24]—you are serving God's honor and glory in many ways.

First, by your present labor and the intention with which you undertake and regulate everything for your neighbor's edification, just as soldiers waiting to get supplies of arms and munitions for the operation about to be launched cannot say that their labor is not in the service of their king. Even if death should overtake one before he begins to work exteriorly for his neighbor, he shall not for that reason have failed in the service of his neighbor, having helped him by the mere fact of his preparation. But besides the intention for the future, he should each day offer himself to God for his neighbor. As God is willing to accept the offering, he can serve as an instrument for the help of his neighbor no less than he would have done by preaching or hearing confessions.

Grow in Virtue, a Necessary Requirement for the Apostolate

The second way is to attain a high degree of virtue, because you will thus be able to make your neighbor such as you are yourselves. For it is God's will that the process of generation observed in material things be observed in things spiritual, *mutatis mutandis.* Philosophy and experience teach us that in the generation of man or animals, besides the general causes such as the heavens, another cause or agent of the same species is required which possesses the same form as that which is to be transmitted, and for this reason it is said that "the sun and man beget man." In like manner, to transmit the form of humility, patience, charity, and so forth, to others, God wills that the immediate cause, which He uses as instrument, such as the preacher or confessor, be humble, charitable, and patient. With the result, as I have said, that, when you benefit yourselves by growing in virtue, you are also of great service to the neighbor.

You are preparing an instrument that is not less, but better, fitted to confer grace by leading a virtuous life than by leading a learned one, although both learning and virtue are required if the instrument is to be perfect.

Give Good Example

The third way of helping the neighbor is by the example of a good life. In this respect, as I have told you, the good odor of your lives has spread abroad and exerts a good influence even beyond the limits of Portugal. I trust that the author of all good will continue His gifts and increase them in you, so that, as you daily grow in perfection, the fragrance of your virtues and the resulting edification will likewise grow, even without your seeking it.

Holy Desires and Prayers

The fourth way of helping your neighbor is very far-reaching indeed, and consists in holy desires and prayers. The demands of your life of study do not permit you to devote much time to prayer, yet you can make up for this by desires, since the time you devote to your various exercises is a continuous prayer, seeing that you are engaged in them only for God's service. But in this and other matters, you have close at hand those who can advise you as to details. Indeed, for that reason part of what I have written could have been omitted, but so seldom do I write to you that I thought I could give myself the consolation of writing at some length.

Conclusion

This is all for the present, except to beg God our Creator and Redeemer that, as it has pleased Him to bestow so great a grace on you as to call you and give you the firm desire of being employed entirely in His service, so He would be pleased to continue and increase His gifts in all, so that you will persevere unwaveringly and grow in His service to His greater honor and glory and the help of His Church.

    From Rome,
    Yours in our Lord,
        Ignatius

6. TO THE FATHERS AND BROTHERS IN PADUA

On Feeling   Rome,
the Effects of Poverty   August 7, 1547

The founder of the college in Padua was Andrea Lippomani, Prior of Santissima Trinità in Venice. When Ignatius spent 1536 in Venice, waiting for his companions to arrive from Paris, he lived with Lippomani and used Lippomani's library to continue his theological studies. Greatly impressed by the work of the young Society, Lippomani offered the revenue from the Priory of the Magdalena in Padua, and half of that of Santissima Trinità to be used to found a Jesuit college in

Padua. The first Jesuits went there in 1542. Five years after its foundation the community was suffering the effects of poverty; the financial assistance promised by Lippomani proved to be inadequate and the Jesuits were in dire want. Pedro de Ribadeneira,[18] a student at Padua writing to Ignatius two months after the community had received Ignatius's letter, describes the typical meals of the community: "First, as to our table. It is usually this: at noon a little vegetable soup and a little meat, that's all! When fruit is in season, we get a few grapes or something else according to the time of year. At night it is the same, a hodge-podge cooked with chicory or something similar, and a little meat. Master Polanco[19] can tell you better, as there has been no change since he left. Although the doctor says that the scholastics must have veal or mutton, this cannot be done, for veal is very high here, as in Rome, and mutton is not butchered in winter, so we must do the best we can with beef." Though the letter to the community at Padua had been drafted by Polanco, Ignatius's secretary, the ideas are those of Ignatius. In the letter he consoles his sons, telling them that poverty is equally a gift from God and should be willingly embraced as any other divine gift. The letter was written in Italian and though the date at the end is given as August 6, 1547, the date at the head of the letter in Ep. 1:572–77, is that of August 7.

May the grace and true love of Jesus Christ be ever in our hearts and increase from day to day to the very end of our lives. Amen.

Dearly beloved fathers and brothers in Christ:

A letter addressed to Father Master Laínez[20] in Florence has come to us through the hands of our and your friend, Pietro Santini. In it we learn, among other things, of the love of poverty, of that poverty which you have chosen for the love of the poor Christ, and the opportunity you sometimes have of suffering some lack of necessities owing to the inadequacy of the help offered you by the kind and charitable prior of the Trinità.

It is not necessary to exhort to patience those who are mindful of their state who keep before their eyes the naked Christ on His cross. And this is especially true since it is clear from the aforementioned letter what a welcome this poverty is given by all of you when you experience its effects. And yet since our Father Ignatius, who has a true father's affection for you, has entrusted me with the task of writing to you, I will console myself, while consoling all of you, with this grace which His Infinite Goodness allows both you and us of feeling the effects of that holy poverty. I have no means of knowing how high a degree of this grace is yours, but with us it is in a very high degree, quite in keeping with our profession.

I call poverty a grace because it is a very special gift from God, as Scripture says: *poverty and riches are from God* [Sir. 11:14]. How much God loved it His only-begotten Son has shown us, who, *coming down from the kingdom of heaven* [Wis. 18:15], chose to be born in poverty and to grow up in it. He loved it, not only in life, suffering hunger and thirst, *without any place to lay His head* [Matt. 8:20], but even in death, wishing to be despoiled of everything, even His clothing, and to be in want of everything, even of water in His thirst.

Wisdom which cannot err wished to show the world, according to Saint Bernard,[21] how precious a jewel is poverty, the value of which the world did not know. He chose it for Himself, so that His teaching, *blessed are they that hunger and thirst, blessed are the poor* [Matt. 5:3, 6] etc. should not be out of harmony with His life.

Christ likewise showed us the high esteem He had for poverty in the choice and employment of His friends, who lived in poverty, especially in the New Testament, beginning with His most holy Mother and His apostles, and continuing on with so many Christians through the course of the centuries up to the present, vassals imitating their king, soldiers their captain, and members their head, Jesus Christ.

So great are the poor in the sight of God that it was especially for them that Jesus was sent into the world: *because of the misery of the needy and the groans of the poor, now will I arise, says the Lord* [Ps. 12:5]. And elsewhere, *he has anointed me to preach the gospel to the poor* [Luke 4:18], words which our Lord recalls when He tells them to give as answer to Saint John, *the poor have the gospel preached to them* [Matt. 11:5]. Our Lord so preferred the poor to the rich that He chose the entire college of His apostles from among the poor, to live and associate with them, to make them princes of His Church and set them as judges over the twelve tribes of Israel—that is, over all the faithful—and the poor will be His counselors. To such a degree has He exalted the state of poverty!

Friendship with the poor makes us friends of the eternal King. Love of poverty makes kings even on earth, kings not of earth but of heaven. And this can be seen in that the kingdom of heaven is promised in the future to others. To the poor and to those who suffer persecution for justice's sake, Immutable Truth promises it for the present: *blessed are the poor in spirit, for theirs is the kingdom of heaven* [Matt. 5:3]. Even in this world they have a right to the kingdom.

And not only are they kings, but they share their kingdom with others, as our Lord teaches us in Saint Luke, *make friends for yourselves with the mammon of iniquity, that when they fail you, a lasting dwelling will be yours* [16:9]. These friends are the poor, particularly the voluntary poor, through whose merits they who help them enter the tabernacles of glory. For they, according to Saint Augustine, are the least of all,[22] of whom our Lord says, *as long as you did it to one of these my least brethren, you did it to me* [Matt. 25:40].

In this, therefore, we see the excellence of poverty which does not stoop to make a treasure of the dunghill or of worthless earth, but with all the resources of its love buys that precious treasure in the field of the Church, whether it be our Lord Himself or His spiritual gifts, from which He Himself is never separated.

But if you consider the genuine advantages which are properly to be found in those means that are suited to help us attain our last end, you will see that holy poverty preserves us from many sins, ridding us as it does of the occasion of sin, for "poverty has not wherewith to feed its love."[23] It slays the worm of riches, which is pride; cuts off the infernal leeches of lust and gluttony, and many other sins as well. And if one should fall through weakness, it helps him to rise at once. For it has none of that attachment which, like a band, binds the heart to earth and to earthly things and deprives us of that ease in rising and turning once more to God. It enables us better to hear in all things the voice—that is, the inspiration—of the Holy Spirit by removing the obstructions that hinder it. It gives greater efficacy to our prayers in the sight of God because *the Lord*

27

will hear the desire of the poor [Ps. 10:17]. If poverty is in the spirit, then the soul is filled with every virtue, for the soul that is swept free of the love of earthly things shall in the same proportion be full of God, having received His gifts. And it is certain that it must be very rich, for God's promise is at the rate of hundred to one, even in this life. The promise is fulfilled even in a temporal sense, when that is for our good. But in the spiritual sense it cannot fail of fulfillment. Thus it is inescapable that they, who freely make themselves poor in earthly possessions, shall be rich in the gifts of God.

This same poverty is "that land fertile in strong men,"[24] as the poet said in words which are truer of Christian poverty than Roman. This poverty is the furnace which tests the progress of fortitude and other virtues and the touchstone which distinguishes genuine gold from counterfeit. It is also the moat which renders secure the camp of our conscience in the religious life; it is the foundation on which the edifice of perfection should rise, according to the words of our Lord, *If you wish to be perfect, go, sell what you have, and give to the poor...and come, follow me* [Matt. 19:21]. It is the mother, the nurse, the guardian of religion, since it conceives, nourishes, and preserves it; while, on the other hand, an abundance of temporal possessions weakens, corrupts, and ruins it. Thus we can easily see the great advantage and the excellence of holy poverty, especially since it is poverty that wins salvation from Him who *will save the poor and the humble* [Ps. 18:27], and obtains for us the eternal kingdom from the same Lord, who says that the kingdom of heaven belongs to the poor, an advantage that is beyond all comparison. So, no matter how hard it may happen to be, holy poverty should be accepted voluntarily.

But really it is not hard; rather it is the cause of great delight in him who embraces it willingly. Even Seneca[25] says that the poor man laughs with greater ease because he has no cares to upset him, a truth which daily experience shows us in the instance of the wayside beggar. If you were to observe the satisfaction in his life, you would see that he is more cheerful than the great merchants, magistrates, princes, and other persons of distinction.

If this is true of people who are not poor by choice, what shall we say of those who are poor because they choose to be? For, neither possessing nor loving anything earthly which they could lose, they enjoy a peace that is imperturbable and a tranquility that is supreme. On the other hand, riches are, for those who possess them, like the sea that is tossed by the storm. Moreover, these voluntary poor, through the peace and security of their conscience, enjoy an uninterrupted cheerfulness which is like a endless banquet. They prepare themselves in a very special way by this very poverty, for heavenly consolations usually abound in the servants of God in proportion as they lack an abundance of the goods and the comforts of earth; if they know how to fill themselves with Christ, He will make up for everything and will occupy, in their hearts, the vacancy left by all else.

But I must not pursue this further. Let what I have said suffice for your consolation and mine to encourage us to love holy poverty, remembering that the excellence, advantage, and joy I have mentioned belong only to that poverty which is lived and willingly embraced, not to the poverty that is accepted because it cannot be avoided. I will add only this, that those who love poverty should, as occasion offers, love her retinue which consists of poor meals, poor clothes, poor sleeping accommodations, and to be held of little account. Whoever loves poverty and is unwilling to feel want, or any of its effects, would be a very finicky poor man and would give the impression of one who loved the name rather than the reality, of one who loved in words rather than in the depth of his heart.

That is all for the present, except to ask our Lord, our Master and true model of spiritual poverty, to grant us all the gift of this precious heritage, which He bestows on His brothers and coheirs, to the end that the spiritual riches of His grace abound in us, and at the end, the ineffable riches of His glory. Amen.

From Rome, August 6, 1547.

7. TO FRANCISCO DE BORJA, DUKE OF GANDÍA

On Prayer and Penance

Rome,
September 20, 1548

Francisco de Borja,[26] *Duke of Gandía, secretly pronounced his vows in the Society on February 1, 1548. Ever since his wife's death in May 1546, he lived a vibrant spiritual life, and now in 1548 he was making plans to resign his title so that he could fully live as a Jesuit. In preparation for that day, he attended the theological course at the Jesuit college in Gandía, which he had founded in 1545, and it is to these studies that Ignatius refers. In a letter to Ignatius, now lost, the duke asked the founder for his opinion on the prayers and penances he was practicing. In his response Ignatius instructs Borja to reduce his prayers, spend more time in study, and to care for his health. The original letter was written in Spanish [Ep. 2:233–37].*

JHS

My lord in our Lord:

May the perfect grace and everlasting love of Christ our Lord be always in our favor and help.

When I hear how harmoniously you have reconciled your spiritual and temporal interests and directed them to your spiritual progress, I find fresh reason, I assure you, for rejoicing in our Lord; and while giving thanks to His Eternal Majesty I can attribute my joy only to His Divine Goodness, which is the source of all our blessings. And yet I realize in our Lord that at one time we may need some exercises, spiritual as well as corporal, and at another time others. Because those which have proved profitable for a time may cease to be so later, I will tell you what I think in His Divine Majesty on this subject, since your lordship has asked for my views.

First. I should think that the time set aside for these exercises, both interior and exterior, should be reduced by half. We ought to increase these exercises when our thoughts have their origin in ourselves or are suggested by our enemy, and lead us to fix our attention on objects that are distracting, frivolous, or forbidden, or when we wish to prevent our wills from taking any satisfaction in them or yielding any consent. I say, as a rule, that as these thoughts multiply we ought to increase our exercises, both interior and exterior, so that we may overcome them, always keeping in mind the individual's character, the varying nature of the thoughts or temptations, and being careful to adapt the exercises to the capacity of the individual. However, when these thoughts weaken and die out, holy thoughts and inspirations will take their place; these we must warmly welcome by opening to them all the doors of the soul. As a result there will be no further need of so many weapons to overthrow the enemy.

From what I can judge of your lordship in our Lord, it would be better if you were to devote to study about half the time you now give to these exercises. In the future, learning will always be very necessary or certainly useful; and not only that which is infused but also that which is acquired by study. Some of your time should go to the administration of your estates and to spiritual conversation. Try to keep your soul always in peace and quiet, always ready for whatever our Lord may wish to work in you. It is certainly a higher virtue of the soul, and a greater grace, to be able to enjoy the Lord in different times and different places than in only one. We should, in the Divine Goodness, strive to attain this.

Second. As to fasts and abstinences, I would advise you in our Lord to strengthen your stomach and your other physical powers, rather than to weaken them. My reason is that, in the first place, when a soul is so disposed to lose its own life rather than offend God's majesty by even the slightest deliberate sin and is, moreover, comparatively free from the temptations of the world, the flesh, and the devil (a condition of soul which I am sure your lordship by God's grace enjoys), I should like very much to see your lordship imprint on your soul the truth that since both body and soul are gifts from your Creator and Lord, you should give Him a good account of both. To do this you must not allow your body to grow weak; for if you do, the interior man will no longer be able to function properly. Therefore, though I once highly praised fasting and abstinence, even from many ordinary foods, and for a certain

31

period was pleased with this program, I cannot now praise it when I see that the stomach, because of these fasts and abstinences, cannot function naturally or digest any of the ordinary meats or other items of diet which contribute to the proper maintenance of the body.

I should rather have you seek every means of strengthening the body. Eat, therefore, whatever food is allowed, and as often as you find it convenient; but it should be done without offense to the neighbor. We should love the body insofar as it is obedient and helpful to the soul, since the soul, with the body's help and service, is better disposed for the service and praise of our Creator and Lord.

Third. Concerning the harsh treatment of the body for our Lord's sake, I would say, avoid anything that would cause the shedding even of a drop of blood. If His Divine Majesty has given you the grace for this and for all that I have mentioned (it is my conviction that He has), it would be better in the future, without listing here any reasons or arguments, to drop this penance, and instead of trying to draw blood seek more immediately the Lord of all, or what comes to the same, seek His most holy gifts, such as the gift of tears. This could arise (1) because of our own sins or the sins of others; or (2) while contemplating the mysteries of the life of Christ, either here on earth or in heaven; or (3) from a loving consideration of the three Divine Persons. Thus the higher our thoughts soar, the greater will be their worth. The third is more perfect than the second, and the second more perfect than the first. But for a given individual the level on which our Lord communicates more of Himself in His holy graces and spiritual gifts will be the best level, because He sees and knows what is best for you. Like one who knows all, He points out the way to you. On our part, with the help of His grace, we will learn by testing many methods, so that we may advance along the way that stands out clearest, which will be for us the happiest and most blessed in this life, leading us directly by ordered paths to that other everlasting life, after having united us in a close embrace with His most holy gifts. By these gifts I understand those that are beyond the reach of our own powers, which we cannot attain at will, since they are rather a pure gift of Him who bestows them who alone can give every good. These gifts, with His Divine Majesty as their end, are an increase in the intensity of faith, hope, and charity, joy and spiritual repose, tears, intense consolations, elevation of mind, divine enlightenments and illuminations, together with all other spiritual relish and understanding which have these gifts as their objects, such as a humble reverence for our holy mother the Church, her rulers, and teachers.

Any of these holy gifts should be preferred to exterior and visible manifestations, which are good only when they have one or other of these higher gifts as their object. I do not mean to say that we should seek them merely for the satisfaction or the pleasure they give us. We know, however, that without them all our thoughts, words, and actions are of themselves tainted, cold, disordered; while with them they become clear, warm, and upright for God's greater service. It is therefore that we should desire these gifts, or some of them, as well as spiritual graces; that is insofar as they are a help to us to God's greater glory. Thus, when the body falls ill because of excessive effort, it is most reasonable to seek these gifts by acts of the understanding and other more moderate exercises. It is not the soul alone that should be healthy; if the mind is healthy in a healthy body, all will be healthy and much better prepared to give God greater service. On how you should act in individual cases, I do not think it wise in the Lord to speak in detail. It is my hope that the same Divine Spirit who has up to now guided your lordship will continue to guide and rule you in the future, to the greater glory of His Divine Majesty.

8. TO THE FATHERS DEPARTING FOR GERMANY

Practical Norms

Rome,
September 24, 1549

In early 1549, Wilhelm IV, Duke of Bavaria, sent a request to Pope Paul III asking for three Jesuits to teach at the University of Ingolstadt. Ever since the death of Johann Eck[27] in 1543, the university had declined in the quality of

*professors and in the number of students. Wilhelm intended
to keep the university a bastion against the Reformation, as it
had been during the days of Eck, and thus he requested the
Jesuits to help restore the university to its former prestige.
Since the duke had already been acquainted with Claude
Jay,[28] who had once taught at Ingolstadt, the duke asked for
him by name and desired two others. Pope Paul sent the
duke's request on to Ignatius, who agreed to send Jay, Alfonso
Salmerón, and Peter Canisius[29] to Germany. Both Canisius
and Salmerón were called from the college in Messina, and as
the group was about to depart Rome, Ignatius drafted a list of
instructions indicating how they were to act and what should
be their goal. Their first task was to be of service to the
university, but Ignatius also felt that they were to see to the
spiritual needs of the people of the city suffering from the
inroads made by Lutheranism, and to look ahead to the
possibility of starting a Jesuit college there. On their way
north the three Jesuits stopped at Bologna to take their
doctorate, which they successfully did on October 4, and
arrived in Ingolstadt on November 13. What is given below is
only the first part of the instruction which was originally
written in Latin [Ep. 12:240–42].*

Jhs

1. Your first and greatest asset will be to distrust yourself and have a great and magnanimous trust in God. Join to this an ardent desire, enkindled and sustained by obedience and charity, to attain the end proposed. Such a desire will keep the end always before your mind, and make you also commend it to God in your sacrifices and prayers and to make diligent use of all other suitable means.

2. The second means is a good life, and therefore an exemplary life. You should shun, not only evil but the very semblance of evil, and show yourselves as patterns of modesty, charity, and all other virtues. Since Germany is in great need of good example, she will derive much help from it; and even though this example be wordless, the affairs of the Society will prosper and God will do battle for us.

3. You should cherish a genuine affection for everyone and

show it to everyone, especially to those who have greater influence over the common good, as the duke himself, to whom you should offer your excuses for arriving so late, and to whom you must show an affection which not only the Apostolic See but our Society cherishes for him as well. Courteously promise him that you will devote your every effort and endeavor to help his people.

4. Show your love in truth and in action by bestowing favors on many, offering them spiritual assistance, and also in exterior works of charity, as will be explained later.

5. Give proof that you are not seeking your own interests, but those of Jesus Christ [Phil. 2:21], that is, His glory and the good of souls. In keeping with this, accept no stipends for Masses or sermons or the administration of the sacraments. You must have no income of any kind.

6. Make yourselves loved by your humility and charity, *becoming all things to all men* [1 Cor. 9:22]. Show that you conform, as far as the Institute of the Society permits, to the customs of the people, and whenever possible see to it that no one goes away from you sad, unless it be for the good of his soul. But do not gratify others at the expense of conscience, and let not excessive familiarity breed contempt.

7. Do not take sides in faction and party strife, but follow a middle course and be friendly with both sides.

8. It will be helpful if you are known to hold sound doctrine both as representatives of the Society and as individuals. This should be with everybody, but especially with the duke and men of influence. It will greatly enhance your reputation not only to cultivate interior composure, but also to manifest it exteriorly: namely, in manner of walking, gestures, appropriate clothing, and above all in circumspection of speech, the maturity of your advice on both practical matters and speculative questions as well. This maturity will keep you from giving your opinion too hastily if the matter is difficult. In such a case take your time to think the matter over, study the question, and even discuss it with others.

9. You must try to be on good terms with those in governmental positions and be kindly disposed toward them. It will help to this if the duke and those members of his household, who have a wide influence, confess to Ours, and insofar as their duties permit, make the Spiritual Exercises. You should win over the professors at the

university and other persons of authority by your humility, modesty, and obliging services.

10. Consequently, if you should learn that you or the Society is in ill esteem, especially with persons in authority, you should prudently undertake a defense, and try to get them to understand the work of the Society and your own, to God's greater glory.

11. It will help to have an exact knowledge of the disposition and character of the men involved, and to consider beforehand all possibilities, especially in matters of importance.

12. It will help if all the companions not only think and speak alike but even dress alike, and observe the same external manners and social customs.

13. Each of the companions should be careful to reflect on what is adapted to the end proposed, and they should talk matters over among themselves. The superior, after having heard what the others think, shall decide what is to be done or left undone.

14. They should write to Rome to ask advice, and to describe conditions. This should be done frequently, as it can be of no little help to all.

15. From time to time they should read this instruction and what will be stated later, and other points which they think ought to be added, so that their memory may be refreshed should it begin to grow dim.

9. TO THE JESUITS IN THE ROMAN HOUSES

On Prompt and
Blind Obedience

Rome,
August 24, 1550

Ignatius personally ordered that this directive on obedience be sent to all the Jesuit houses in Rome. The obedience that Ignatius expected from his sons was to be prompt and blind. The basic idea expressed in this instruction is likewise enshrined in the Constitutions of the Society of Jesus, *Part VI, chap. 1. The original directive was written in Italian [Ep. 3:156–57].*

Our reverend Father Master Ignatius wishes for God's greater glory and the greater spiritual progress of all of Ours (as he has already partly declared in other ordinances), that in the future, when his reverence or father minister summons anyone, whether he be a priest or not, or the subminister calls one who is not a priest, they should all answer the call at once, as though it was the voice of Christ our Lord, and practice this obedience in the name of His Divine Majesty. In this way obedience should be blind and prompt. If one is at prayer, he should leave his prayer. If he hears the voice of his superior, or rather the voice of Christ our Lord, when he is writing and has begun a letter, say *A* or *B*, he should not wait to finish it.[30]

In like manner, if he happens to be with anyone at all, even a prelate (supposing he owes him no obedience), he should come if he is called by any of his superiors. Should one be called who happens to be taking some bodily refreshments of any kind, whether he be at table or in bed, or busy with an invalid, serving a drink or a medicine, or engaged in a service which could not be interrupted without harm to the patient, such as helping to bleed him, or should he be going to confession or about to receive Communion, or hearing the confessions of others, if a priest, in all such cases he should send word to the superior and ask whether he wishes him to leave his meal, or his bed, or whatever else it may happen to be.

Given at Rome, August 24, 1550.

10. TO THE MEMBERS OF THE SOCIETY GATHERED IN ROME

Ignatius Submits His Resignation

Rome, January 30, 1551

By 1550 the Spanish text of the Society's Constitutions was complete and Ignatius summoned many of the older professed fathers to Rome to discuss it. The meetings lasted from early January to February 1, 1551, and as the meetings were drawing to an end Ignatius, on January 30, 1551, presented to the assembled fathers, a sealed letter containing his resignation as general of the Society. Of all the fathers only one[31] thought that whatever Ignatius desired should be done. The others, however, were unanimous in maintaining that they would have no one else as general while Ignatius was alive. This message was sent to Ignatius, who humbly accepted their decision and remained general until his death in 1556. Ignatius composed this letter in Spanish [Ep. 3:303-4].

Ihus

1. At different times throughout these months and years I have given this matter free and undisturbed thought, and I will state, in the presence of my Creator and Lord, who is also my eternal judge, what I take to be the balanced results of this reflection, to the greater praise and glory of the Divine Majesty.

2. Regarding calmly and with a sense of reality what I see in myself, as a result of my many sins, imperfections, and infirmities of body and soul, I have often and at different times come to the conclusion that I really do not possess (in fact, I infinitely lack) the gifts required for the proper discharge of the office which the Society itself has laid on me.

3. I have a great desire in our Lord that this matter be taken under consideration, and that another who is better, or not so bad, take over the office of governing the Society which is now mine.

38

4. I desire that such a person be chosen and given this office.

5. And not only does my desire persist, but I think with good reason that this office should be given, not only to one who would perform it better, or not so poorly, but to one who would have at least equal success.

6. Considering all this, in the name of the Father, and of the Son, and of the Holy Spirit, my one and only God and Creator, I lay down and renounce simply and absolutely the office which I hold, and beg and beseech in our Lord with all my heart, both the professed and those who wish to join them, to be pleased to accept this resignation which is made with so much sincerity before His Divine Majesty.

7. If those who are to accept and pass judgment on this petition to God's greater glory detect any inconsistency in it, I beg of them for God's love and reverence to commend it to His Divine Majesty, so that in all things His most holy will be done to His greater glory and to the greater general good of souls and of the whole Society, understanding everything for the greater praise and eternal glory of God.

Rome, this day, Friday, January 30, 1551.

Ignatius

11. TO FATHER ANTONIO BRANDÃO

On Aspects
of the Spiritual Life

Rome,
June 1, 1551

When Simão Rodrigues,[32] Portuguese provincial, traveled to Rome in the last months of 1550 to be present at the discussions on the Constitutions, Antonio Brandão[33] was one of the Jesuits who accompanied him. The group, however, only arrived in the Eternal City on February 8, 1551, a week after the discussions had come to an end. While in Rome Brandão, who was a priest-scholastic at the time, took the opportunity to leave a list of fifteen questions with Polanco,

Ignatius's secretary, with the request that Ignatius give his opinion on those points. Brandão and Rodrigues left Rome in the spring to return to Portugal, but it was not until June 1 that Ignatius sat down to answer his questions. The queries dealt with practical aspects of the spiritual life, that is, prayer, Mass, confession, fraternal correction, and so on. Ignatius's answer is a description of the way he thought scholastics ought to be trained. Though the thoughts expressed in this response are those of Ignatius, the response was written by Polanco in Spanish [Ep. 3:506–13].

Jhs

Instructions given by our Father Ignatius, or under his direction, for those living outside Rome, as well as on other points worthy of notice and which should not be forgotten.

For Portugal

A scholastic of the Society wishes to have our father's directives on the following points:

1. How much time should be given to prayer by one still in studies, and how much time should he spend conversing with his brothers, supposing that the rector has set no limits to these activities?

2. Should Mass be celebrated daily, or only on certain days, even when it seems a hindrance to study?

3. After finishing philosophy should one give more time to speculative or to moral theology, the supposition being that one does not give oneself entirely to both these subjects in college?

4. What is to be done when one finds oneself entertaining an inordinate desire for knowledge?

5. Should one offer oneself to the superior before being asked to do a certain task, or should one leave the entire matter in his hands?

6. What method of meditation, more in keeping with our vocation, should be followed?

7. In confession, should one get down to particular imperfections or, for the sake of brevity, be satisfied with mentioning the more general faults?

8. If confession is made to a member of the community and the confessor questions the penitent, even though there is no question of sin, in what instances should the confessor ask the penitent's permission to inform the superior of the content of the confession?

9. What attitude should one take in speaking with the superior concerning the difficulties of others? Should he make a complete revelation of them, even though some of them have ceased to be troublesome?

10. Should one correct an imperfection noticed in a member of the Society, or should it be allowed to pass, allowing the individual to be deceived into thinking that it is no imperfection?

11. If, before God, one believes that the superior—the rector, for instance—is wrong in a certain matter, should the provincial be informed, and the same of other subordinate superiors, or should one close one's eyes?

12. What rule should be followed in writing either to externs or to Ours, when there is no real need, nor having been commanded to do so, but merely out of motives of charity?

13. In dealing with externs or Ours, should they use language which might appear to them to be mere civility, or should they avoid all forms of flattery?

14. What should one do about volunteering information concerning one of the Society, and how should it be done?

15. Would it be lawful to counsel an extern, or one of the house without vows, to take vows?

What should they do about using or not using a privilege of the Society in dealing with a penitent?

The first question has two parts, and the answer to the first part is to remember that the purpose of a scholastic at a college is to study, to acquire that knowledge with which he can serve God's greater glory and be of help to his neighbor. This is a task which demands all that a man has, and he will not give himself completely to his studies if he also gives a large amount of his time to prayer. Hence it will be sufficient if scholastics who are not priests (supposing there is no interior trial or exceptional feeling of devotion), give one hour to prayer over and above Mass. During Mass the scholastic should make a short meditation while the priest is at the secret parts, but during the hour of prayer he would ordinarily recite the hours of our Lady or some other prayer, or meditate, should the rector judge this to be better. If the scholastic is a priest, it will be enough for him to say his office, celebrate Mass, and make the examens. Should his devotion move him, he could add another half hour.

The second part of the question will be answered if we consider the goal of conversing with others, which is to influence for good him with whom we converse. This edification is hindered by excess in either direction, and we should therefore avoid extremes and try to hold a middle course.

With respect to the last clause of this question, our reverend father made some remarks on the great esteem we should have for obedience. Some saints have excellences that are wanting in others, and the same is true of religious orders; and therefore it was his desire that in the Society there be an excellence, which would put it on a footing with any other religious order, even if they had excellences which we could not aspire to equal, though we might well make the attempt in some things—poverty, for instance. But our reverend father wished that our excellence be obedience; we have a greater obligation to excel in it because of the extra vow of obedience which the fathers have to the sovereign pontiff, which takes away every excuse we might have for not carrying out an order of obedience. And he also said that this obedience could not be perfect unless the understanding of the subject was in complete conformity with the understanding of the superior. Without this conformity life would be a continual purgatory, and with little hope of stability.

To the second question our reverend father answered that, considering the purpose one of Ours should have in his studies, he could be satisfied with two Masses a week, over and above Sundays and feast days, supposing that none of the three following reasons urge otherwise, (1) obedience, (2) common good, (3) exceptional devotion.

To the third question, preference should be given to speculative theology, because, after finishing college, one has to devote oneself to moral theology, since that is necessary in speaking with

42

others, and speculative theology is proper to class work where one studies fundamental truths.

The fourth question will be answered with the sixth.

The fifth. It would be good to offer oneself once for all to the superior for him to direct to the greater glory of God our Lord, leaving all care of oneself to him who has the place of Christ our Lord on earth, seldom making any representation unless something occurs which might especially require it.

The sixth. Considering the goal of our studies, the scholastics can hardly give themselves to prolonged meditations. Over and above the spiritual exercises assigned for their perfection—namely, daily Mass, an hour for vocal prayer and examen of conscience, and weekly confession and Communion—they should practice the seeking of God's presence in all things, in their conversations, their walks, in all that they see, taste, hear, understand, and in all their actions, since His Divine Majesty is truly in all things by His presence, power, and essence. This kind of meditation, which finds God our Lord in all things, is easier than raising oneself to the consideration of divine truths which are more abstract and which demand something of an effort, if we are to keep our attention on them. But this method is an excellent exercise to prepare us for great visitations of our Lord, even in prayers that are rather short. Besides this, the scholastics can frequently offer to God our Lord their studies and the efforts they demand, seeing that they have undertaken them for His love to the sacrifice of their personal tastes, so that to some extent, at least, we may be of service to His Divine Majesty and of help to the souls for whom He died. We can also make these exercises the matter of our examen.

To these exercises we may add that of preaching in the colleges. After the example of a good life, one of the most efficient means of helping the neighbor, and one which is especially fitting to the Society, is preaching. Our reverend father was of the opinion that no little fruit could be gathered if the scholastics did some preaching. He thought they should preach on Sundays, on subjects of their own choosing, and as an exercise that involves no loss of time, two or three of them could, during supper, recite the tones[34] which they had been taught, using, in the beginning, the formula that is in use here in Rome. Then as things evolve another could easily be adopted which could develop according to local customs.

The advantages of this exercise are very great, but for brevity's sake we omit mentioning them here.

The seventh deals with confession. To avoid any mistake, we should notice from which side the enemy begins his attack and tries to make us offend our Lord. If he aims at getting us to commit mortal sins easily, the penitent should weigh well even the least imperfections which lead to that sin, and confess them. If he finds himself drawn to doubts and difficulties, seeing sin where there is no sin, he should not descend into minute details, but only mention his venial sins, and of these only the more important ones. If by God's grace the soul is at peace with God our Lord, let him confess his sins briefly, without going into detail. He should try to feel shame for them in God's presence, considering that He who is offended is infinite, which imparts a kind of infinity to the sin. But by the sovereign goodness of God our Lord they are venial, and are forgiven by using a little holy water, striking one's breast, making an act of contrition, and so forth.

To the first part of the eighth, questions may and sometimes should be raised regarding certain venial faults, for they may be the means of revealing mortal sins and help the penitent to a clear manifestation of his conscience, by which he may be further helped.

The second part of the eighth question. For greater clarity on this point, our father insisted on the importance of the superior's being in touch with all that concerns his subjects, so that he could provide for each one according to his needs. Thus, if he knows that one is undergoing temptations of the flesh, he will not station him near fire by assigning him, for example, to hear the confessions of women, and so forth. Nor will he entrust government to one who is lacking in obedience. To guard against anything like this happening, our father usually reserves certain cases to himself; all mortal sins, for example, and vehement temptations against the Institute, the superior, and other forms of instability. Keeping this in mind the confessor, according to the circumstances of each case, may discreetly ask leave to make a manifestation to the superior. There is reason to believe that, in this way, a troubled conscience will be helped more in the Lord than in any other.

The ninth. The answer to the ninth may be deduced from the preceding, and it is that the superior should be wholly informed about everything, even of things past, always taking for granted one's good will, and with every precaution for the due observance of charity toward the neighbor.

The first part of the tenth concerns correcting another. For this to be successful, it will help much if the corrector has some authority, or acts with great affection, an affection that can be recognized as such. If either of these qualities is absent, the correction will fail; that is, there will be no amendment. For this reason it would not be proper for everybody to undertake such correction. But in whatever manner it is done, and if one is reasonably certain that it will be well taken, one's admonition should not be too forthright, but toned down and presented without offense. Since one sin leads to another, it is quite possible that, once committed, the sin will not dispose the sinner to accept even a well-intentioned correction in the right spirit.

To the second part of the tenth, as to whether one should be left under the false impression that there is no imperfection, our reverend father says that it might be better for the person's progress to do so. The more one attends to the faults of others, the less he will see of his own and, thus, make less progress himself. But if one is really advancing with his passions well under control and in good order, with our Lord expanding his heart so that he is a help to others as well as to himself, such a one may correct him who is in error, provided the manner suggested in number eleven be followed.

As an answer to the eleventh question, our father recounted what he told the first fathers after the six of them had made their profession together; namely, that they could help him toward perfection in two ways: the first was their own perfection; the second was to call his attention to whatever they thought was contrary to this perfection in him. He wanted them to have recourse to prayer before they corrected him and, then, if in the presence of God our Lord there was no change in their understanding and judgment, they were to tell him privately, a procedure which he himself follows now. Our father said that it would be a great help to success in this matter if the superior entrusted this duty to some of his subjects—priests, for example, and others who are respected. He who wishes only to benefit himself would do well to close the eyes of his judgment. If anyone should have something to say, let him first carefully place himself in the presence of our Lord, so as to know and make up his mind what he ought to do. Second, he should find some acceptable way of telling the delinquent if he thinks that he will accept the correction. But if he thinks that he will not accept it, let him tell the superior. Our father thought it would be a great advantage to have a syndic to make these things known to the superior. Besides, he would have one or two as vice-rectors, one subject to the other, to help the rector, and with this arrangement the rector would be better able to be of greater help to one or the other and would keep the affection of his subjects, since they could look upon him as a refuge if they thought themselves severely dealt with by the vice-rectors.

Our father gave an answer to the thirteenth which seems rather striking to me; namely, that in dealing with another we should take a cue from the enemy who wishes to draw a man to evil: he goes in the way of the one whom he wishes to tempt, but comes out his own way. We may thus adapt ourselves to the inclinations of the one with whom we are dealing, adapting ourselves in our Lord to everyone, only later to come out with the good accomplished to which we had laid our hand. Our father made another remark as to how to free oneself from one whom there was no hope of helping. He suggests talking to him rather pointedly of hell, judgment, and such things. In that case he would not return; or if he did, the chances are that he would feel himself touched in our Lord.

Finally, one should accommodate oneself to the character of him with whom one is dealing, whether he be phlegmatic, choleric, and so forth. But this should be done within limits.

The remaining questions depend more on the circumstances of individual cases, which, in this instance, were not given.

12. TO FATHER ANTONIO ARAOZ

On Caring for
One's Health

Rome,
June 1, 1551

Antonio Araoz[35] was the nephew of Ignatius's sister-in-law, Magdalena de Araoz, wife of Martín García, an elder brother of Ignatius. Araoz was the first Spanish Jesuit to work in Spain; he proved to be an indefatigable laborer for the Lord and, as provincial, he established many new houses of the Society. He had been in Rome for the discussions on the Constitutions and had returned to Spain in April 1551. Ignatius received word that Araoz was not eating properly, could not sleep, and that he was suffering from so great a weakness that his physician ordered him to return to his native air to convalesce. In earlier letters Ignatius had paternally recommended that he take better care of his health, but in the present letter Ignatius chose to be more explicit, that is, he commands him under holy obedience to take three months off and do nothing but obey the physician's orders. Ignatius wrote this letter in Spanish [Ep. 3:534–35].

JHS

May the sovereign grace and everlasting love of Christ our Lord ever be our help and support.

I have been informed of the great need you have to look after your health, something I have partially known. I do know that, though your health is frail, you allow yourself to be carried away by your charity to undertake tasks and labors that are more than you can conveniently bear. Judging in God our Lord that it would be more acceptable to His Divine Majesty to have you temper your zeal in this respect so that you will be able to labor the longer in his service, I have deemed it proper in our Lord to command you to follow the physician's advice in all that pertains to your meals, the use of your time, what hours and when you are to take for sleep and repose. For the next three months, from now until September, you are to do no preaching, but are to look after your health. An occasional exception may be made, if in the opinion of our lord, the duke, or of Don Juan,[36] you can do so once a month without injury to your health. To avoid any contrary interpretation, and that you may know that I really mean this in our Lord, I command you in virtue of holy obedience to do as I here direct.

I beg God our Lord to give us all His bountiful grace ever to know His most holy will and perfectly to fulfill it.

From Rome, June 1, 1551.

13. TO FATHER JEAN PELLETIER

On Ministering to the Neighbor

Rome, June 13, 1551

The Jesuit college in Ferrara was opened in 1551. In mid-May of that year, Ignatius assigned eight Jesuits—three priests and five scholastics—to Ferrara, the rector of the group was Jean Pelletier.[37] Within weeks of their departure from Rome, Ignatius sent Pelletier an instruction describing the Jesuit manner of proceeding with regard to ministering to the neighbor. This is one of the most complete instructions of Ignatius on this theme. The document has three parts. In the first Ignatius deals with the preservation and increase of the Society and suggests the following means: purity of intention, obedience to superiors, regular observance, preaching, study, and spiritual conversations. The second part treats the manner of giving edification to the faithful and gathering spiritual fruit, and here Ignatius lists the principal ministries to be employed in dealing with externs. The third part tells the Jesuits to show good will to the reigning prince and recommends that they secure an endowment and a site for a house. This instruction, written in Italian [Ep. 3:542–50], was also sent to the newly established colleges in Modena, Florence, and Naples.

IHS

Instruction on the Way of Proceeding

There are three objectives you should keep in mind. One is the preservation and increase of the Society in spirit, learning, and numbers. The second is that we should look to the edification of the city and seek spiritual fruit in it. The third is to consolidate and increase the temporalities of the new college, so that our Lord will be better served in the first and the second objectives.

Part I

The first objective, which regards membership in the Society, is something of a foundation for the others, because the better the workers are, the more suitable they will be to be accepted by God as instruments for the edification of externs and the continuation of the foundation.

1. To this end all should have a right intention, so that they will seek solely, not their own interests but *the things that are Jesus Christ's* [Phil. 2:21]. They should endeavor to conceive great resolves and elicit equally great desires to be true and faithful servants of God, and to render a good account of themselves in that which has been laid upon them, with a true abnegation of their own will and judgment and a total submission of themselves to God's government of them by means of holy obedience. And this, whether they are employed in important offices or in tasks of little moment. They should, as far as possible, be fervent in their prayers to obtain this grace from him who is the giver of all good. The superior should occasionally remind them of this duty.

2. As far as possible, the order and method of this Roman College should be followed, especially in the practice of weekly confession and Communion, in the daily examination of conscience and the hearing of Mass in the house, if they have a chapel, and if not, elsewhere if it seems expedient; in the practice of obedience and the avoidance of dealings with externs, except as the rector shall direct. The latter will decide how much responsibility is to be entrusted to each for the edification of others, without danger of loss to himself.

3. In the community refectory there should be a daily exercise in preaching, one after the other, either at dinner or supper. This exercise may be either ex tempore or prepared, but not more than an hour should be given to its preparation. In addition to this there should be weekly preaching in the vernacular or in Latin. For this a subject should be proposed on which one will speak without preparation. There should also be sermons in Greek. Or they may have the tones. This second item, however, may be changed and adapted to the abilities of the students.

4. Let each one be intent on his progress in learning and in helping his companions, and give himself to study or lecturing which the rector shall indicate. Care must be taken that the lectures are accommodated to the capacity of the students. All should be well grounded in grammar and be trained in composition, the masters being careful to correct all themes. There should be some practice in discussions and debates. There should be sufficient opportunity to have all this done at home without having recourse to extern schools. Some, however, may be sent to these schools if the superior, taking all circumstances into account, should think it proper.

5. In all these literary and spiritual associations they should try to win others to the life of perfection. With younger students this should be tried only with the greatest skill. Even the older among them should not be received into our schools without their parents' consent. However, should it be thought expedient to receive one of these into our house after he has firmly expressed his resolve, or to send him to Rome or elsewhere, this may be done. Discretion and the unction of the Holy Spirit will point out the best course. But in case of doubt one may, to make certain, write to the provincial or to Rome.

6. The better to attain these ends it will be good to have some of the more advanced students carefully compose Latin discourses on some Christian virtue, such as may be seen in the list of subjects that has been drawn up, and have them declaim them publicly in everyone's presence, on Sundays and feast days. Young men and others, especially those who seem to have some aptitude for the religious life, could be invited to hear them. This is a suitable way of preparing those whom the Savior is inviting to walk the road to perfection. At the very least they will be giving good example and

edification, and the members of the community will be helped in the practice of letters and of virtue.

Part II

With regard to the second objective, namely, attending to the edification and spiritual profit of the city, you should, besides helping those outside the Society with prayers and the example of modesty and virtue, make some effort to do so by means of the following external practices.

1. Teach Latin and Greek to all who come to you, according to their native ability, and even Hebrew, and let the students exercise themselves in composition and in debating.

2. Care should be taken to teach children their catechism on all Sundays and feast days, and even during the week, following the order of the Roman College or another that may be thought more suitable. This could be done in the house or in some convenient and nearby place, which you may judge to be better adapted for the purpose.

3. Be very careful to have the students form good habits. If possible, see that they attend Mass daily, and they should hear a sermon on feast days when one is scheduled. They should confess once a month, and avoid all oaths as well as all blasphemous and indecent speech.

4. If it can conveniently be done, there should be a sermon on Sundays and feast days, or one of them might explain the catechism.

5. If it can be done, a lecture on Holy Scripture or scholastic theology should be given for priests, such as something on the sacraments or some cases of conscience.

6. Special attention should be given to heresies, and you should be properly armed against them. Keep in mind the subjects that are most attacked by the heretics, and try to be considerate in laying bare their wounds and applying a remedy. If this much cannot be done, then their false teaching must be opposed.

7. You should try to bring people to the sacraments of penance and Communion, and be ready to administer them.

8. You will be able to help all with whom you deal if you make

use of spiritual conversations, especially if you find your hearers disposed to benefit from them. The first week of the Exercises can be given to anyone; but the other weeks only to those whom you find suitable for the state of perfection and who truly desire to be helped.

9. You should be careful to help prisoners and visit the prisons if you can, and you should occasionally preach and exhort them to confession and a return to God. Hear their confessions if opportunity offers.

10. Do not forget the hospitals. Try to console and give spiritual help to the poor as far as you can. Even in these places some exhortation may be profitable, unless circumstances seem to advise otherwise.

11. In general you should try to keep informed about the pious works in the city where you reside, and do all you possibly can to help them.

12. Although many means of helping the neighbor and pious works are here proposed, discretion will be your guide in the choice you must make. It is taken for granted that you cannot do all of them, but you should never lose sight of the greater service of God, the common good, and the good name of the Society.

Part III

The third objective deals with consolidating and increasing the temporal goods of the new college. A great help toward this will be the daily sacrifices and the special prayers which all the members of the community ought to offer for this purpose, insofar as it will be for God's glory. Moreover, the observance of what has been said in the first and second objectives will help more than any other means we could devise. But to touch on a few means belonging properly to this third objective, we suggest the following:

1. Try to preserve and increase the prince's good will, and try to please him whenever possible according to God. Serve him in those pious works which he is especially interested in promoting, provided they do no injury to God's service. Likewise, be careful to maintain a good name, esteem, and favor with him, and speak to him in such a way that he will come to hope that the Society is

disposed on its part to help the work progress, even if it usually begins in a small way, so that later it may grow rather than fail.

2. You will also have to make an effort to win over individuals and benefactors, and talk with them about spiritual things. To help them in a special way is something quite proper and acceptable to God, with whose business we are concerned.

3. The better to preserve your own authority in spiritual matters, you should try, if possible, to have our friends, rather than ourselves, make the requests for us and manage our temporal affairs; or let it be done in such a way that there is no appearance of greed. To avoid all such worries, it might be better to settle on a fixed amount for your support. Nothing should be said about this, except at the proper time and in the proper manner.

4. Have a special care that, though it may not be offered at present, a good site may be offered in time that will be sufficiently large, or one which can be added to until it is large enough, for a house, a church, and a school, and, if possible, not far from the center of the city.

5. Write to us every week for help and guidance.

14. TO FATHER CLAUDE JAY

On the Study of Theology
Rome, August 8, 1551

While attending the Diet of Augsburg (1550), Claude Jay succeeded in interesting several of the German princes, but especially Ferdinand I, King of the Romans, to promote Catholic reform in their territories. Moved by Jay's words and knowing of the success that the Jesuits had in Ingolstadt, Ferdinand decided to invite the Jesuits to Vienna. With this in mind the king wrote to Pope Julius III, asking that Jay and several other Jesuit theologians be sent to the University of Vienna to help reinstate a faculty of Catholic theology. Since the Reformation the university had ceased teaching courses in Catholic theology, and Ferdinand, brother of Emperor Charles V, was one of the few German princes who did not favor the Protestant movement. Ignatius wrote to Ferdinand in April 1551 [Ep. 3:401-2], expressing his happiness that the Society could be of some service in restoring theological courses at the university and promised to send several Jesuits to Vienna. Jay arrived in the Austrian capital on April 25, and began teaching; in July he wrote[38] to Ignatius asking the founder's opinion how they should go about establishing a theological faculty. In his response Ignatius describes three ways by which such a faculty could be instituted, but after explaining the first and second ways he lists the difficulties that such ways would have in Germany, and thus suggests a third, a middle course way. Important in this letter is Ignatius's conviction that the study of theology demands thorough preparation both in languages and philosophy. The original instruction was written in Italian [Ep. 3:602-5].

Jhs

May the grace and peace of Christ our Lord ever grow in our souls.

From your reverence's letter of July 21 our Father Master Ignatius has learned of the holy desire that his majesty the king has of reforming theological studies in the University of Vienna, in fact, of restoring them, since, as we understand, they have been practically given up since there were no students enrolled in the courses. Considering the conditions of the times in Germany, this foresight on the part of the king certainly seems to be highly desirable and especially necessary. Our father, and indeed all of us, would consider it a privilege to help his majesty in this matter if the Society is able. But I will frankly inform your reverence of what is thought here about the means to attain this end—that is, the restoration of theological studies in Vienna—and you can make what representation you think proper to his majesty.

If we give the matter serious thought, three ways present themselves. The first way is the one which your reverence says his majesty wishes to use; namely, that every province send several students for theology, that some of these be Jesuits, and that there be frequent lectures and lessons, and so forth. This program would be feasible, it seems, if a large number of students could be found in Vienna or could come in from the provinces, who are prepared to begin theology and to follow through to the end. Such an arrangement would be necessary for the success of this plan. But there is reason to fear that these conditions are lacking, and that on two counts.

The first is, as we have learned, that there is today little inclination and interest among the Germans for such study, especially for scholastic theology. Without this interest and inclination every class exercise will prove boring, and in the end there will be little progress. The other reason is that such students, even though they be well disposed, will not have the proper foundation in logic and philosophy, or even perhaps in languages. Such a foundation is indispensable. If some students are found, they will be very few in number; and for a program in theology a large number of fit and well-grounded students is needed. Otherwise, as experience in other universities teaches, the whole thing will catch a chill and die. It is not enough to establish a good program if there is no one to follow it and, in the end, we will not attain the end we have in view. If it is said that our own scholastics could form the nucleus, there would not be enough of them and others might get the idea that they ought to leave theology to religious. Thus they will never attain the goal of supplying parishes with educated pastors, since Ours cannot undertake such parishes. The first way would seem, then, to be beset with these difficulties.

The second way is to begin more methodically to prepare students, keeping in mind the ultimate purpose of restoring the study of theology. This would be to have the provinces send on young men who are destined for this study. They should first be well grounded in Latin, and those who have the ability and are thought capable, in Greek and Hebrew as well. After a good foundation in the humanities a large number, say a hundred or so, should begin the course in liberal arts and be carefully trained in it. In subsequent years others who have been well grounded in the humanities will enter the course in good numbers. But they should always keep theology in mind, and the teachers of the humanities and philosophy should constantly encourage them and fill them with a love for theology. When they have finished their philosophy, of the hundred who began, perhaps fifty or more will be ready for theology. If they have come in sufficient numbers, are well disposed to theology, and have laid a good foundation in the lower branches, their progress will be noticeable.

This would seem to be a very good way, but certain difficulties may be encountered. The first is that the result of so much labor will be long in coming, even though a matter of four or six years should not be considered long when we think of the permanence of the result. The second is that there are already many students in the university advanced in languages, and some even in philosophy, who would not be disposed to give themselves to the lower branches. The third is that it would not seem very becoming in a university like that of Vienna to omit the higher branches even for a time while the students were being grounded in the lower.

A third way could be taken which would avoid these difficulties, and it is this. Let the lectures in philosophy and theology continue as they now are, but insist, as was indicated in the second way, and make it a point to do so, on laying a good foundation for the future study of theology. The students in the lower classes of languages should be instructed and prepared so that the students, who come from the provinces to study theology as well as the others who are now attending the university studying languages, see to it that they get a good foundation in the liberal arts under teachers who will try to enkindle in them a desire for sacred theology and a love for it. Once there is a goodly number of young men who have advanced in the study of languages, they could begin a course in philosophy, seriously and diligently after the manner of Paris. Thus in the following years, when they have finished the course of arts or philosophy, there will be a good number of well-trained students eager for theology. This will be the time to begin a course in theology, and later, as the years pass on, it could be given as it is at Paris. Public lecturers will then draw a large attendance and an audience able to profit from them.

In this last way the college which his majesty the king is preparing for the Society can be of no small help, because, in the first place, it will offer lecturers in humanities and languages who, besides their lectures, will have a special care to see that the students are exercised and advance in their studies and in good morals, and are inspired with a longing for the study of theology.

Once the college has a competent number of well-prepared students, it can also supply lecturers in philosophy who will proceed as we have indicated, and make their students ready for theology. And after these are prepared, it will be able in the same way to supply teachers of theology who will carry on their courses after the manner of Paris, where our Society first made its studies and with whose teaching methods it is acquainted.

This way seems to be free from objections. The first difficulty mentioned above, the delay, can be better endured, especially since it is necessary and does not entail any interruption in the ordinary lectures of the university. The second difficulty, which deals with students already advanced, ceases for the same reasons, because, if they do not wish to lay a better foundation they can go on as they are doing. The third, the danger to the reputation of the university ceases for the reason that everything will continue as usual. If some lecturers leave and there are no others to replace them, one could be provided from the college for a course in Sacred Scripture, and another for cases of conscience, and so on, until there are students sufficiently well prepared, as we have indicated, to begin a course in scholastic theology with a good foundation. This might seem to be laying a heavy burden on the Society, to provide lecturers in humanities and later on in philosophy and theology, but we are under such heavy obligations to his majesty the king, and the public good resulting will be so great, that we should in no way hold back.

Your reverence, therefore, should take up this whole matter with the bishop of Laibach,[39] and if he approves, with his majesty the king. Our father, by explaining his thoughts and offering to do what he can, is partially repaying a general debt of charity, and a special debt which he owes to the service of his majesty, to the glory of God our Lord. May He in His infinite wisdom guide us all and govern us so as to contribute to the salvation of souls and His praise and glory. Amen.

From Rome.

15. TO FATHER MANUEL GODINHO

On Necessary   Rome,
Temporal Occupations   January 31, 1552

After having been involved in the training of young Jesuits at San Fins, Manuel Godinho[40] was appointed treasurer of the college in Coimbra. Being somewhat rigid and austere in his personal life, he found his new position unnerving since he was now immersed in temporal and financial matters. He felt these occupations nullified any good he might accomplish through his priestly ministry and concluded that these occupations were an obstacle to his growth in perfection. With this in mind he wrote to Ignatius in a letter no longer extant. Ignatius responds by encouraging him and explaining that even the most secular of occupations, when done with a pure intention, is as agreeable to God as is prayer, in fact, even more agreeable when done under obedience. In 1552 Godinho gave up his position as treasurer to take on a more burdensome task as rector of the college. The letter was written in Spanish [Ep. 4:126–27].

May the perfect grace and everlasting love of Christ our Lord ever be in our favor and help.

I received your letter, dear brother in our Lord, and from it I learned of your arrival from San Fins with the brethren who were under your care, and that everything, by the grace of God our Lord, was done with due edification.

Though the charge of temporal affairs seems to be and is distracting, I have no doubt that by your good and upright intention you turn everything you do to something spiritual for God's glory, and are thus very pleasing to His Divine Goodness. The distractions which you accept for His greater service, in conformity with His divine will interpreted to you by obedience, cannot only equal the union and recollection of uninterrupted contemplation, but even be more acceptable to Him, proceeding as they do from a more active and vigorous charity. May God our

Creator and Lord deign to preserve and increase this charity in your soul and in the souls of all. We correctly hold that any activity in which charity is exercised unto God's glory, is very holy and suitable for us, and those actions even more so in which the infallible rule of obedience to our superiors has placed us. May He who gave to Elisha this twofold spirit [2 Kings 2:9], which you say is so necessary, grant it to you in abundance. I will not be negligent in desiring and begging it of His Divine Majesty.

If, looking only to God's glory, you still think that in God's service this office is unsuitable for you, confer with your superiors there, and they will do what is proper. Even here, as one who holds you very close to his heart, I will not fail to help you.

May Christ our Lord help us all with His bountiful grace, so that we may know His holy will and perfectly fulfill it.

From Rome, January 31, 1552.

Yours in our Lord,

Ignatius

16. TO FATHER FRANCISCO DE BORJA

On Declining Ecclesiastical Dignities

Rome, June 5, 1552

Ever since Francisco de Borja[41] resigned his title in May 1551, his cousin, Emperor Charles V, held it unthinkable that a former duke should remain a simple priest and, thus, in March 1552, he proposed to Pope Julius III that Borja become a cardinal. The pope immediately took to the idea and rumors soon spread through Rome. Ignatius heard the rumors but waited to see if they died of themselves or whether they would be confirmed. In the latter part of May the pope mentioned, in one of his consistories, that the emperor had suggested four Spaniards for the cardinalate, and one of these was Borja. Many of the cardinals expressed their happiness in having Borja join their ranks and mentioned this to Ignatius.

16. TO FATHER FRANCISCO DE BORJA

Ignatius was at first disinclined that Jesuits accept ecclesiastical dignities, and so he prayed over the matter for three days. The result was that he was now definitely opposed to the idea and so he went to visit several cardinals and the pope himself. In speaking to his holiness Ignatius maintained that it would be for the greater service and glory of God if Borja were to remain in the humble position that he himself had chosen. The pope was persuaded by Ignatius's reasoning and the matter was dropped. These details are found in the letter that was written by Juan Polanco on June 1, 1552 [Ep. 4:255–58], and mentioned by Ignatius in the letter below. Ignatius wrote his own letter to Borja on June 5, and told him of his reaction when he heard the news about the cardinal's hat, and what he did to prevent it being given him. He also asks Borja to write him and give his own thoughts on the matter. Ignatius penned his letter in Spanish [Ep. 4:283–85].

IHS

May the sovereign grace and everlasting love of Christ our Lord ever be our protection and support.

With regard to the cardinal's hat, I thought that I should give you, for God's greater glory, what I myself experienced, and speak to you as I would to my own soul. When I was informed that it was certain that the emperor had nominated you and that the pope was willing to create you cardinal, I at once had the impulse and the prompting to do all I could to prevent it, and yet, not being certain of God's will, as I saw many reasons for both sides, I gave orders in the community that all priests should celebrate Mass and those not priests to offer their prayers for three days for divine guidance, for God's greater glory. During this period of three days I reflected and talked with others about it and felt certain fears or, at least, not that freedom of spirit to speak out against the appointment and to try to prevent it. I said to myself: "How do I know what God our Lord wishes to accomplish?" Consequently, I did not feel entirely safe in speaking out against it. At other times, as during my usual prayers, I felt that these fears had disappeared. I repeated this prayer at different intervals, sometimes with these fears and sometimes without them, until finally, on the third day, when making my usual prayer, I came to a determination so final, so peaceful and free, that I should do all I could with the pope and cardinals to prevent it. I felt sure at the time and still feel so, that, if I did not act in this manner I would not be able to give a good account of myself to God our Lord—indeed, that I would give quite a bad one.

Therefore I have felt, and now feel, that it is God's will that I oppose this move. Even though others might think otherwise and bestow this dignity on you, I do not see that there would be any contradiction, since the same Divine Spirit could move me to this action for certain reasons and move others to the contrary for still other reasons, and thus bring about the result desired by the emperor. May God our Lord always do what will be to His greater praise and glory. I believe it would be quite fitting for you to answer the letter on this subject which Master Polanco is writing in my name, and declare the intention and purpose with which God our Lord has inspired you and may now inspire you. Your opinion would thus appear in writing and could then be produced whenever it may be called for, leaving the whole matter in the hands of God our Lord, so that His holy will may be done in all our affairs.

Your letter of March 13 will be answered in another letter. May it please God our Lord that your journey and everything else has met with the success we have hoped for in His Divine Majesty, and that you are now in perfect health of body and mind, as I desire and constantly ask God our Lord in my poor unworthy prayers, to the greater glory of His Divine Majesty. May He in His infinite mercy be our constant help and support.

From Rome.

17. TO THOSE SENT TO MINISTER TO OTHERS

Principles for Ministry

Rome,
October 8, 1552

As the Society grew in membership Ignatius found it somewhat easier to send Jesuits, not only to foreign countries, but also to the major European cities where reigning princes had expressed a desire for a Jesuit college to be founded, for example, Ingolstadt, Vienna, Ferrara, Naples, Messina. In October 1552 Ignatius jotted down the principles that ought to guide the Jesuits in their ministries, and he divides his short instruction into three parts: principles concerning oneself, the neighbor, and the Society. Success in the ministry depends on complete purity of soul, faithfulness to exercises of piety, understanding the persons with whom they are to deal, establishing a hierarchy of values among the works they are to perform. At the same time the Jesuits are to be guided by the Holy Spirit and their superiors, and are to try to attract suitable young men to the Society. The headings in the instruction, which was originally written in Italian, have been added [Ep. 12:251-53].

Jhs

Whoever in this Society is sent to labor in the vineyard of the Lord, should keep three things in mind: the first concerns himself, the second concerns the neighbor with whom he deals, and the third, the head and the whole body of the Society of which he is a member.

Principles Concerning Oneself

With regard to the first, that is with respect to himself, he should not be forgetful of himself because of his interest in the neighbor. He should refuse to commit even the slightest sin to further the greatest apostolic gain in the world, and not even place himself in danger of committing one. He will find it a help if he avoids dealing with persons from whom he has reason to fear danger; and if he does deal with them, it should be rarely and in public. He should make little account of external appearances, and look upon creatures not as fair or attractive, but as bathed in the blood of Christ, as images of God, temples of the Holy Spirit, and so on.

He should defend himself from all evil and acquire every virtue; and the more perfectly he possesses them, the more successfully will he be able to draw others to them. To this end, it will be helpful daily to assign some time for the examination of conscience, prayer, and the reception of the sacraments, etc.

He should take into account his own health and his body's strength.

Principles Concerning the Neighbor

With regard to the neighbor, which is the second point, we must be careful with whom we deal. They should be persons from whom we can expect greater fruit, since we cannot deal with everyone. They should be such as are in greater need, and those in high position who exert an influence because of their learning or their temporal possessions; those who are suited to be apostolic workers and, generally speaking, all those who, if helped, will be better able to help others for God's glory.

2. With regard to the works he undertakes, he should prefer those for which he is especially sent, rather than others. Among the other works he should prefer the better, that is, the spiritual to the corporal, the more urgent to the less urgent, the universal to the particular, those that have some permanence to those that are ephemeral, since he cannot do both. We should remember that it is not enough to begin but that we must, as far as possible, finish and insure the endurance of good and pious works.

3. As to the instruments we must use, besides good example and prayer that is full of desires, we must consider whether to make use of confession, the Exercises and spiritual conversations, teaching catechism, or lectures, sermons, and so forth. We should select those weapons (since we cannot use all of them) which will be judged to be more effective and with which we are better acquainted.

4. As to our method of procedure, we should try to be humble by beginning at the bottom and not venturing into lofty subjects unless we are invited or asked to do so, or discretion should dictate otherwise, taking into consideration the time, place, and persons. This discretion cannot be reduced to any hard-and-fast rule. Our method should include an effort to secure the good will of the persons with whom we are dealing by truly manifesting our virtue and affection, and this will command some authority with them. We should make use of holy prudence in adapting ourselves to everyone. This prudence will certainly be taught us by the unction of the Holy Spirit, but we ourselves can assist it by reflection and careful observation. The above-mentioned examination of conscience could be extended to include this consideration, and it should be made at a fixed hour of the day. Special attention should be given to cases of conscience; and when the solutions of these difficulties are not clear in our own minds, we should not hazard an answer or solution, but first give it the study and consideration it requires.

Principles Concerning the Society

With reference to the third point, that is the regard we should have for the head and body of the Society, it is shown principally by allowing oneself to be directed by the superior and by keeping him informed of what he should know and by obediently obeying the orders he shall give.

2. You can serve the good name and reputation of the Society by helping wherever you can for the glory of God, and this will be done especially by encouraging foundations of colleges and particularly, when you see the opportunity, by recruiting acceptable candidates for the Society. These should be persons educated, alert, and young, especially when endowed with good manners, health, intelligence, and who are disposed to good and are free of other impediments, and so on.

18. TO FATHER DIEGO MIRÓ

On Dismissing   Rome,
the Disobedient   December 17, 1552

Diego Miró[42] became provincial in Portugal at the very end of 1551, after Ignatius had removed Simão Rodrigues from that position. This change caused further tension in the province since Rodrigues was mild and easy-going in his governing while Miró was somewhat strict and demanding. The unfortunate result was that some members of the province, siding with Rodrigues, refused to show obedience to the new provincial. Miguel de Torres[43] had been sent by Ignatius to Portugal to see that Rodrigues accepted Ignatius's decision, and to insure a smooth transition for the incoming Miró. During his several months in Portugal, Torres periodically reported to Rome about the lamentable state of affairs in that province. Ignatius would not tolerate disobedience and thus he wrote to Miró instructing him to dismiss from the Society those who refuse to obey, or to send them to Rome if there is hope the change might bring about amendment. He likewise asked him to notify João III, King of Portugal, of this instruction. This letter was written in Spanish [Ep. 4:559–63].

Jhs

May the sovereign grace and everlasting love of Christ our Lord be ever our protection and support.

According to information coming to us from Doctor Torres, whom I sent to the province of Portugal as my representative and visitor in the Lord, I understand that there is a notable failing, among not a few of Ours, in that virtue which is more necessary and essential in the Society than anywhere else, and in which the vicar of Christ, in the bulls of our Institute, most carefully recommends that we distinguish ourselves. I mean the respect, reverence, and perfect obedience to our superiors who hold the place of Christ our Lord, even of His Divine Majesty.

You can realize, from what you have heard, how I should and do desire this virtue in my brothers, and what satisfaction must be mine when I hear that some among you disrespectfully say to their superior, "You should not order me to do this," or "It is not good for me to do this," or, as I am told, that some are unwilling to do what they are told, or that the actions of some show so little reverence and interior submission to the one whom they ought to reverence as the representative of Christ our Lord and, accordingly, humble themselves in all things before His Divine Majesty. This matter seems to have gone so far because of the fault of one whose duty it was to correct it, but who failed to do so. May God our Lord forgive him! How much better it would have been to remove a diseased member from the body of the Society in order to protect the healthy members, than to allow it to remain and infect with so serious a disease many others by example and association. On another occasion I have written how gratified I was that Master Leonard[44] in Cologne had dismissed nine or ten together who had gone wrong. Later he did the same again, which I approved, though if measures had been taken when the trouble began, it might possibly have been enough to dismiss one or two. Now, though late, the remedy is being applied in Portugal. Better late than never!

I command you in virtue of holy obedience to take the following step with regard to the safeguarding of that virtue. If there is anyone who is unwilling to obey you—and I say this, not to you alone but to all superiors or local rectors in Portugal—do one of two things: either dismiss him from the Society, or send him here to Rome if you think that a particular individual can, by such a change, be helped to become a true servant of Christ our Lord. If necessary, keep their highnesses informed, who I doubt will make any objections, in keeping with the spirit and holy good will which God our Lord has bestowed upon them. To retain one who is not a true son of obedience does no good for the kingdom. Nor is there any reason for thinking that such a person, his own soul being so destitute, can help other souls, or that God our Lord would wish to accept him as an instrument for His service and glory.

We see from experience that men, not only with average talents but even less than average, can often be the instruments of uncommon supernatural fruit, because they are completely obedient and through this virtue allow themselves to be affected and moved by the powerful hand of the author of all good. On the other hand, great talent may be seen exerting great labor with less than ordinary fruit, because being themselves the source of their activity, that is, their own self-love, or at least not allowing themselves to be moved by God our Lord through obedience to their superiors, they do not produce results proportionate to the almighty hand of God our Lord, who does not accept them as His instruments. They achieve results proportioned to their own weak and feeble hands. Their highnesses understand this, and I am sure that they will make no difficulty. And while we have enough to do here without burdening ourselves with this additional task from Portugal, we will not decline the added burden because of the special charity which God our Lord causes us to feel toward Portugal.

This is all for the present, except to beg the Divine and Supreme Goodness to give us all His abundant grace to know His most holy will and perfectly to fulfill it.

From Rome, December 17, 1552.

This precept of obedience which I am sending you, requiring you to dismiss those who are disobedient, or to send them here to Rome, is to be published in all the colleges and houses throughout the province. And see that the king is informed of it, so that those who are sent beyond the limits of the kingdom, because they have need of help, do not appear as being withdrawn from Portugal because we here are looking for workers who would otherwise be useful within the territory of his highness. Rather, let it appear that they are being sent elsewhere to prepare them to be such when they return, as his highness desires, as are all the others in the service of God and of souls in his kingdom.

Yours in our Lord,

Ignatius

19. TO THE MEMBERS OF THE SOCIETY IN EUROPE

On Patience
in Practicing Poverty

Rome,
December 24, 1552

Though this letter of Ignatius is brief, nevertheless, it is full of affection as he exhorts his sons to embrace the grace of poverty. To help them accept it with greater readiness and cheerfulness, Ignatius reminds the Jesuits of their brothers in India. The letter was written in Italian [Ep. 4:564–65].

The peace of Christ.

From various letters we learn that God our Lord is visiting your reverences with the effects of holy poverty, that is, the inconveniences that come from being deprived of certain temporal goods which are necessary for health and the body's well-being. It is no small grace that the Divine Goodness deigns to bestow on us in allowing us actually to taste that which we should always desire if we are to walk in the footsteps of our guide Jesus Christ, and in conformity with the vow taken in accordance with the Institute of our holy order.

Truly, I do not know if there is any place in the Society where the members do not have a share in this grace, though one place might feel it more than another. Suppose we compare ourselves with our brothers in India, who, while involved in such corporal and spiritual labors, are so ill provided with food that in some places they do not even have bread, to say nothing of wine for drinking. There they have to get along with a bit of rice and water, or something similar, and as little nourishing. They are ill clothed and have a minimum of bodily comfort. If we compare ourselves with them, I do not think that our suffering is excessively hard. We can also imagine that we are in our own India, which is to be found everywhere. If he who ordinarily provides us with our necessities fails, we can then resort to a holy mendicancy, by which means we can supply our needs. All things considered, if God our Lord wishes that we too have something to suffer, see that nothing is lacking the sick; those in good health will have a better opportunity to exercise patience. May our Lord Jesus Christ, who has made patience so lovable by His teaching and example, give it to us, and may He grant us His love and a relish for His service in preference to everything else.

From Rome, December 24, 1552.

20. TO FATHER DIEGO MIRÓ

On Being Confessors
to Kings

Rome,
February 1, 1553

In July 1552 João III of Portugal requested the new provincial, Diego Miró,[45] to accept the guidance of his conscience, but Miró appealed to a long string of excuses, among them that the king did not know him, that he was a foreigner, a Spaniard, that members of the Society were not permitted to accept such honors or dignities, and that it was more fitting for Jesuits to work among the poor, in the hospitals, and so forth. To all this the king simply replied that he was not asking Miró to abandon his humble labors among the poor, all he was requesting was that he hear his confession, that of Queen Catalina, and of their heir, Prince João. Unable to convince Miró to accept the position the king asked the same of Luis Gonçalves da Câmara,[46] but without success. The question was placed in abeyance until they received Ignatius's views on the subject. The letter below is Ignatius's instruction to both Jesuits, and he clearly tells them that it is the part of the Jesuit vocation to hear confessions and to give Communion to all who come to them, whether they be poor or rich. Ignatius also goes on to answer the several objections that both Jesuits had brought up against accepting the position as the king's confessor, but Ignatius answers each of them. Besides being a duty flowing from the Jesuit calling to dispense the sacraments, Ignatius reminds them that the Society owes a great debt to the king since he most generously founded the college in Coimbra and helps support the Jesuits in India, and was now thinking of a mission to Ethiopia. Ignatius felt that in no way could the Jesuits refuse what the king was now asking of them. When the discussions were over it was Gonçalves da Câmara who became the king's confessor. The letter was written in Spanish [Ep. 4:625-28].

The sovereign and everlasting love of Christ our Lord be ever our help and favor.

From various letters received from Portugal we learn that his highness had asked, with pressing devotion, that you and Father Luis Gonçalves act as his confessors, but that you have both excused yourselves, not on the grounds of conscience or because of scruples in directing his highness, whom you consider a saint, as you say, but because you think that this is an honor which should be refused no less than a bishopric or a royal chaplaincy. For the same reason Father Luis Gonçalves has resigned his post with the prince, I understand.

I can, of course, see your reasons, based on humility and the security which is more easily found in lowly than in prominent occupations, and I can only approve and be edified by your motives. But, all things considered, I am convinced that, when you consider the greater service and glory of God our Lord, you are ill advised in your decision.

In the first place, it is our vocation and in keeping with our Institute to administer the sacraments of confession and Communion to men of all conditions and ages. And the same duty of giving consolation and spiritual help to our neighbor obliges us to care for those in high position as well as those in low.

Secondly, the whole Society, ever since its beginning, is under special obligation to their highnesses, indeed, more than to any other Christian prince, whether we take into account their good works or the special love and charity, which more than anything else, ought to win over your hearts. I cannot think of any excuse that would justify our failure to serve their highnesses in a matter that is so much in keeping with our vocation, and in which they show that they will receive consolation and satisfaction of soul.

Now, if we consider the universal good and God's greater service, even greater good will follow from this, as far as I can see in the Lord, because all the members of the body share in the good of the head and all his subjects in the good of their sovereign, so that the spiritual good which is done to the sovereign should be more highly esteemed than if it were done to others.

Since you judge one instance by another, consider whether there could be a more important memorial left by a confessor than to bring to a conclusion the appointment of the patriarch of Ethiopia,[47] which involves the salvation, not of many souls but of many cities and provinces. Whichever of you acts as his highness's confessor, be sure that you do not fail to come to some understanding on this appointment, and every time you write to Rome be sure to mention this matter and let me know what you have done.

To return to the reasons why you should not refuse this task, I do not think your security of soul is relevant, because if all we looked for in our vocation was to walk safely, and if we had to sacrifice the good of souls in order to get away from danger, we would not be living and associating with our neighbor. But according to our vocation, we deal with everyone, rather as Saint Paul says of himself, *we should make ourselves all things to all men* [1 Cor. 9:22] to gain all to Christ; and if we advance with a pure and upright intention, seeking not our own interests *but those of Jesus Christ* [Phil. 2:21], He Himself in His infinite goodness will be our protection. If our vocation did not take a firm hold on His powerful hand, it would not be enough for us merely to withdraw from such perils to keep from falling into others that are perhaps greater.

Whatever people may say about your seeking honor and position will collapse of itself under the weight of the truth and the evidence of the work when they see that you retain the lowliness that you have chosen for Christ our Lord. And so, for whatever the crowd might think or say, you should not neglect anything than can be turned to the service of God, or of their highnesses, and the common good.

Finally, to satisfy my conscience once and for all in this matter, I command you in virtue of holy obedience, you and Father Luis Gonçalves, to do what their highnesses bid you in this matter; that is, one or the other of you, unless someone else in the Society appears better qualified to you and at the same time is acceptable to his highness. Have confidence in the Divine Goodness that whatever is done in this matter under obedience will be for the best. You must make this command known to his highness, and show him this letter should he wish to see it or at least give him a summary of it.

As Master Polanco is going to write at length on other matters, I will say no more here except to commend myself to your prayers and sacrifices. I beg God our Lord to give us all His bountiful grace always to know His most holy will and entirely to fulfill it.

From Rome, February 1, 1553.

Yours in our Lord,

Ignatius

21. TO THE MEMBERS OF THE SOCIETY IN PORTUGAL

On Perfect Obedience
Rome,
March 26, 1553

This letter on obedience is Ignatius's most celebrated and most widely-read letter. As early as 1545 Ignatius heard of certain shortcomings among the Jesuits in the Portuguese province with regard to obedience; the news that his sons were acting in a manner entirely foreign to the spirit of the Society brought him great distress. The sad condition in Portugal was largely due to the easy-going style of government of its provincial, Simão Rodrigues. So popular was he among some that the province developed factions, and the group favoring Rodrigues was attached to him with an affection that was far from spiritual. The problem became so acute that Ignatius found it necessary to remove Rodrigues and appoint a new provincial, Diego Miró. But as long as

Rodrigues remained among his followers, the new provincial could do nothing to turn the province around. Disobedience was still rampant and Ignatius wrote to Miró in December 1552,[48] instructing him to dismiss from the Society any and all who disobeyed his orders.

In January 1553 Luis Gonçalves da Câmara[49] wrote to Ignatius from Lisbon[50] and described the sorrowful state of the province where the subjects have become the real superiors, and urgently requested Ignatius to write to his sons in Portugal and share with them his thoughts on obedience. Two months later Ignatius acceded to this request. Ignatius's letter studies the question of obedience in depth. He first states that obedience is to be the characteristic virtue of the Society and then goes on to speak of its fundamental principle, its three degrees, suggests practical ways of acquiring it, and ends by exhorting his sons to strive to attain it. Ignatius intended his letter to remedy the disorders in Portugal and within months after its arrival Rodrigues decided to leave Portugal and by the end of 1553 peace was again restored to the province. This letter [Ep. 4:669–81] was drafted by Polanco and was written in Spanish with the several patristic citations given in Latin. The headings in the letter below have been added to facilitate reading.[51]

Jhus

May the perfect grace and everlasting love of Christ our Lord greet and visit you with his most holy gifts and spiritual graces.

1. Obedience Is To Be the Characteristic Virtue of the Society

It gives me great consolation, my dear brothers in our Lord Jesus Christ, when I learn of the lively and earnest desires for perfection in His divine service and glory which He gives you, who by His mercy has called you to this Society and preserves you in it and directs you to the blessed end at which His chosen ones arrive.

And though I wish you all perfection in every virtue and spiritual gift, it is true (as you have heard from me on other occasions), that it is in obedience, more than in any other virtue, that God our Lord gives me the desire to see you signalize yourselves. And that, not only because of the singular good there is in it, so much emphasized by word and example in Holy Scripture in both Old and New Testaments, but because, as Saint Gregory says: "obedience is the only virtue which plants all the other virtues in the mind, and preserves them once they are planted."[52] And insofar as this virtue flourishes, all the other virtues will flourish and bring forth the fruit which I desire in your souls, and which He claims who, by His obedience, redeemed the world after it had been destroyed by the lack of it, *becoming obedient unto death, even death on a cross* [Phil. 2:8].

We may allow ourselves to be surpassed by other religious orders in fasts, watchings, and other austerities, which each one following its institute holily observes. But in the purity and perfection of obedience together with the true resignation of our wills and the abnegation of our understanding, I am very desirous, my dear brothers, that they who serve God in this Society should be conspicuous, so that by this virtue its true sons may be recognized as men who regard not the person whom they obey, but in him Christ our Lord, for whose sake they obey.

2. The Foundation of Obedience

The superior is to be obeyed not because he is prudent, or good, or qualified by any other gift of God, but because he holds the place and the authority of God, as Eternal Truth has said: *He who hears you, hears me; and he who rejects you, rejects me* [Luke 10:16]. Nor on the contrary, should he lack prudence, is he to be the less obeyed in that in which he is superior, since he represents Him who is infallible wisdom, and who will supply what is wanting in His minister; nor, should he lack goodness or other desirable qualities, since Christ our Lord, having said, *the scribes and the Pharisees sit on the chair of Moses*, adds, *therefore, whatever they shall tell you, observe and do; but do not act according to their works* [Matt. 23:2-3].

Therefore I should wish that all of you would train yourselves to recognize Christ our Lord in any superior, and with all devotion, reverence and obey His Divine Majesty in him. This will appear less strange to you if you keep in mind that Saint Paul, writing to the Ephesians, bids us obey even temporal and pagan superiors as Christ, from whom all well-ordered authority descends: *Slaves, obey those who are your lords according to the flesh, with fear and trembling, in singleness of heart, as to Christ, not serving to the eye as pleasers of men, but as the slaves of Christ doing the will of God from your heart, giving your service with good will as to the Lord and not to men* [Eph. 6:5-7]. From this you can judge, when a religious is taken not only as superior, but expressly in the place of Christ our Lord, to serve as director and guide in the divine service, what rank he ought to hold in the mind of the inferior, and whether he ought to be looked upon as man or rather as the vicar of Christ our Lord.

3. Degrees of Obedience
Obedience of Execution and of the Will

I also desire that this be firmly fixed in your minds, that the first degree of obedience is very low, which consists in the execution of what is commanded, and that it does not deserve the name of obedience, since it does not attain to the worth of this virtue unless it rises to the second degree, which is to make the superior's will one's own in such a way that there is not merely the effectual execution of the command, but an interior conformity, whether willing or not willing the same. Hence it is said in Scripture, *obedience is better than sacrifice* [1 Sam. 15:22], for, according to Saint Gregory, "In victims the flesh of another is slain, but in obedience our own will is sacrificed."[53]

Now because this disposition of will in man is of so great worth, so also is the offering of it, when by obedience it is offered to his Creator and Lord. How great a deception it is, and how dangerous for those who think it lawful to withdraw from the will of their superior, I do not say only in those things pertaining to flesh and blood, but even in those which of their nature are spiritual and holy, such as fasts, prayers, and other pious works! Let them hear Cassian's comment in the Conference of Daniel the Abbot: "It is one and the selfsame kind of disobedience, whether in earnestness of labor, or the desire of ease, one breaks the command of the superior, and as harmful to go against the statutes of the monastery out of sloth as out of watchfulness; and finally, it is as bad to transgress the precept of the abbot to read as to contemn it to sleep."[54] Holy was the activity of Martha, holy the contemplation of Magdalene, and holy the penitence and tears with which she bathed the feet of Christ our Lord; but all this was to be done in Bethany, which is interpreted to mean, the house of obedience. It would seem, therefore, that Christ our Lord would give us to understand, as Saint Bernard remarks, "that neither the activity of good works, nor the leisure of contemplation, nor the tears of the penitent would have pleased Him out of Bethany."[55]

And thus my dear brothers, try to make the surrender of your wills entire. Offer freely to God through his ministers the liberty He has bestowed on you. Do not think it a slight advantage of your free will that you are able to restore it wholly in obedience to Him who gave it to you. In this you do not lose it, but rather perfect it in conforming your will wholly with the most certain rule of all rectitude, which is the divine will, the interpreter of which is the superior who governs you in place of God.

For this reason you must never try to draw the will of the superior (which you should consider the will of God) to your own will. This would not be making the divine will the rule of your own, but your own the rule of the divine, and so distorting the order of His wisdom. It is a great delusion in those whose understanding has been darkened by self-love, to think that there is any obedience in the subject who tries to draw the superior to what he wishes. Listen to Saint Bernard, who had much experience in this matter: "Whoever endeavors either openly or covertly to have his spiritual father enjoin him what he himself desires, deceives himself if he flatters himself as a true follower of obedience. For in that he does not obey his superior, but rather the superior obeys him."[56] And so he concludes that he who wishes to rise to the virtue of obedience must rise to the second degree, which, over and above the execution, consists in making the superior's will one's own, or rather putting off his own will to clothe himself with the divine will interpreted by the superior.

Obedience of the Understanding

But he who aims at making an entire and perfect oblation of himself, in addition to his will, must offer his understanding, which is a further and the highest degree of obedience. He must not only will, but he must think the same as the superior, submitting his own judgment to that of the superior, so far as a devout will can bend the understanding.

For although this faculty has not the freedom of the will, and naturally gives its assent to what is presented to it as true, there are, however, many instances where the evidence of the known truth is not coercive and it can, with the help of the will, favor one side or the other. When this happens every truly obedient man should conform his thought to the thought of the superior.

And this is certain, since obedience is a holocaust in which the whole man without the slightest reserve is offered in the fire of charity to his Creator and Lord through the hands of His ministers. And since it is a complete surrender of himself by which a man dispossesses himself to be possessed and governed by divine providence through his superiors, it cannot be held that obedience consists merely in the execution, by carrying the command into effect and in the will's acquiescence, but also in the judgment, which must approve the superior's command, insofar, as has been said, as it can, through the energy of the will bring itself to this.

Would to God that this obedience of the understanding were as much understood and practiced as it is necessary to anyone living in religion, and acceptable to God our Lord. I say necessary, for as in the celestial bodies, if the lower is to receive movement and influence from the higher it must be subject and subordinate, the one body being ordered and adjusted to the other; so when one rational creature is moved by another, as takes place in obedience, the one that is moved must be subject and subordinated to the one by whom he is moved, if he is to receive influence and energy from him. And, this subjection and subordination cannot be had unless the understanding and the will of the inferior is in conformity with that of the superior.

Now, if we regard the end of obedience, as our will so our understanding may be mistaken as to what is good for us. Therefore, we think it expedient to conform our will with that of the superior to keep it from going astray, so also the understanding ought to be conformed with his to keep it from going astray. *Rely not on your own prudence* [Prov. 3:5], says Scripture.

Thus, they who are wise judge it to be true prudence not to

rely on their own judgment even in other affairs of life, and especially when personal interests are at stake, in which men, as a rule, because of their lack of self-control, are not good judges.

This being so, we ought to follow the judgment of another (even when he is not our superior) rather than our own in matters concerning ourselves. How much more, then, the judgment of the superior whom we have taken as a guide to stand in the place of God and to interpret the divine will for us?

And it is certain that this guidance is all the more necessary in men and matters spiritual, as the danger in the spiritual life is great when one advances rapidly in it without the bridle of discretion. Hence Cassian says in the Conference of the Abbot Moses: "By no other vice does the devil draw a monk headlong, and bring him to death sooner, than by persuading him to neglect the counsel of the elders, and trust to his own judgment and determination."[57]

On the other hand, without this obedience of the understanding it is impossible that the obedience of will and execution be what they should be. For the appetitive powers of the soul naturally follow the apprehensive and, in the long run, the will cannot obey without violence against one's judgment. When for some time it does obey, misled by the common apprehension that it must obey, even when commanded amiss, it cannot do so for any length of time. And so perseverance fails, or if not this, at least the perfection of obedience which consists in obeying with love and cheerfulness. But when one acts in opposition to one's judgment, one cannot obey lovingly and cheerfully as long as such repugnance remains. Promptitude fails, and readiness, which are impossible without agreement of judgment, such as when one doubts whether it is good or not to do what is commanded. That renowned simplicity of blind obedience fails, when we call into question the justice of the command, or even condemn the superior because he bids us do something that is not pleasing. Humility fails, for although on the one hand we submit, on the other we prefer ourselves to the superior. Fortitude in difficult tasks fails, and in a word, all the perfections of this virtue.

On the other hand, when one obeys without submitting one's judgment, there arise dissatisfaction, pain, reluctance, slackness, murmurings, excuses, and other imperfections and obstacles of no small moment which strip obedience of its value and merit.

Wherefore Saint Bernard, speaking of those who take it ill when commanded to do things that are unpleasant, says with reason: "If you begin to grieve at this, to judge your superior, to murmur in your heart, although outwardly you fulfill what is commanded, this is not the true virtue of patience, but a cloak for your malice."[58]

Indeed, if we look to the peace and quiet of mind of him who obeys, it is certain that he will never achieve it who has within himself the cause of his disquiet and unrest, that is, a judgment of his own opposed to what obedience lays upon him.

Therefore, to maintain that union which is the bond of every society, Saint Paul earnestly exhorts all *to think and say the same thing* [1 Cor. 1:10], because it is by the union of judgment and will that they shall be preserved. Now, if head and members must think the selfsame, it is easy to see whether the head should agree with the members, or the members with the head. Thus, from what has been said, we can see how necessary is obedience of the understanding.

But how perfect it is in itself, and how pleasing to God, can be seen from the value of this most noble offering which is made of the most worthy part of man; in this way the obedient man becomes a living holocaust most pleasing to His Divine Majesty, keeping nothing whatever to himself; and also because of the difficulty overcome for love of Him in going against the natural inclination which all men have of following their own judgment. It follows that obedience, though it is a perfection proper to the will (which it makes ready to fulfill the will of the superior), yet, it must also, as has been said, extend to the understanding, inclining it to agree with the thought of the superior, for it is thus that we proceed with the full strength of the soul—of will and understanding—to a prompt and perfect execution.

4. General Means for Attaining Obedience

I seem to hear some of you say, most dear brothers, that you see the importance of this virtue, but that you would like to see how you can attain to its perfection. To this I answer with Pope Saint Leo, "Nothing is difficult to the humble, and nothing hard to the meek."[59] Be humble and meek, therefore, and God our Lord will bestow His grace which will enable you to maintain sweetly and lovingly the offering that you have made to Him.

5. Particular Means for Attaining Obedience

In addition to these means, I will place before you three especially which will give you great assistance in attaining this perfection of obedience.

Seeing God in the Superior

The first is that, as I said at the beginning, you do not behold in the person of your superior a man subject to errors and miseries, but rather him whom you obey in man, Christ, the highest wisdom, immeasurable goodness, and infinite charity, who, you know, cannot be deceived and does not wish to deceive you. And because you are certain that you have set upon your own shoulders this yoke of obedience for the love of God, submitting yourself to the will of the superior in order to be more conformable to the divine will, be assured that His most faithful charity will ever direct you by the means you yourselves have chosen. Therefore, do not look upon the voice of the superior, as far as he commands you, otherwise than as the voice of Christ, in keeping with Saint Paul's advice to the Colossians, where he exhorts subjects to obey their superiors: *Whatever you do, do it from the heart, as serving the Lord, and not men, knowing that you will receive from the Lord the inheritance as your reward. Serve the Lord Christ* [3:23-24]. And Saint Bernard: "whether God or man, his substitute, commands anything, we must obey with equal diligence, and perform it with like reverence, when however man commands nothing that is contrary to God."[60] Thus, if you do not look upon man with the eyes of the body, but upon God with those of the soul, you will find no difficulty in conforming your will and judgment with the rule of action which you yourselves have chosen.

Seeking Reasons to Support the Superior's Command

The second means is that you be quick to look for reasons to defend what the superior commands, or to what he is inclined, rather than to disapprove of it. A help toward this will be to love whatever obedience shall enjoin. From this will come a cheerful obedience without any trouble, for as Saint Leo says: "It is not hard to serve when we love that which is commanded."[61]

Blind Obedience

The third means to subject the understanding which is even easier and surer, and in use among the holy Fathers, is to presuppose and believe, very much as we are accustomed to do in matters of faith, that what the superior enjoins is the command of God our Lord and His holy will. Then to proceed blindly, without inquiry of any kind, to the carrying out of the command, with the prompt impulse of the will to obey. So we are to think Abraham did when commanded to sacrifice his son Isaac [Gen. 22:2-3]. Likewise, under the new covenant, some of the holy Fathers to whom Cassian refers, as the Abbot John, who did not question whether what he was commanded was profitable or not, as when with such great labor he watered a dry stick throughout a year.[62] Or whether it was possible or not, when he tried so earnestly at the command of his superior to move a rock which a large number of men would not have been able to move.[63]

We see that God our Lord sometimes confirmed this kind of obedience with miracles, as when Maurus, Saint Benedict's disciple, going into a lake at the command of his superior, did not sink.[64] Or in the instance of another, who being told to bring back a lioness, took hold of her and brought her to his superior.[65] And you are acquainted with others. What I mean is that this manner of subjecting one's own judgment, without further inquiry, supposing that the command is holy and in conformity with God's will, is in use among the saints and ought to be imitated by any one who wishes to obey perfectly in all things, where manifestly there appears no sin.

6. Representation

But this does not mean that you should not feel free to propose a difficulty, should something occur to you different from his opinion, provided you pray over it, and it seems to you in God's presence that you ought to make the representation to the superior. If you wish to proceed in this matter without suspicion of attachment to your own judgment, you must maintain indifference both before and after making this representation, not only as to undertaking or relinquishing the matter in question, but you must even go so far as to be better satisfied with, and to consider as better, whatever the superior shall ordain.

7. Final Observations

Now, what I have said of obedience is not only to be understood of individuals with reference to their immediate superiors, but also of rectors and local superiors with reference to provincials, and of provincials with reference to the general, and of the general toward him whom God our Lord has given as superior, his vicar on earth. In this way complete subordination will be observed and, consequently, union and charity, without which the welfare and government of the Society or of any other congregation would be impossible.

It is by this means that Divine Providence gently disposes all things, bringing to their appointed end the lowest by the middlemost, and the middlemost by the highest. Even in the angels there is the subordination of one hierarchy to another; and in the heavens, and all the bodies that are moved, the lowest by the highest and the highest in their turn unto the Supreme Mover of all.

We see the same on earth in well-governed states, and in the hierarchy of the Church, the members of which render their obedience to the one universal vicar of Christ our Lord. And the better this subordination is kept, the better the government. But when it is lacking everyone can see what outstanding faults ensue. Therefore, in this congregation, in which our Lord has given me some charge, I desire that this virtue be as perfect as if the whole welfare of the Society depended on it.

8. Final Exhortation

Not wishing to go beyond the limits I set at the beginning of this letter, I will end by begging you for the love of Christ our Lord, who not only gave us the precept of obedience, but added His example, to make every effort to attain it by a glorious victory over yourselves, vanquishing the loftiest and most difficult part of yourselves, your will and understanding, because in this way the true knowledge and love of God our Lord will possess you wholly and direct your souls throughout the course of this pilgrimage,

until at length He leads you and many others through you to the
last and most happy end of bliss everlasting.

From Rome, March 26, 1553.

The servant of all in our Lord,

Ignatius

22. TO THE WHOLE SOCIETY

Prayers for Germany   Rome,
and England   July 25, 1553

*Peter Canisius,[66] writing to Ignatius from Vienna, sometime
in June or July 1553, asked him to request Masses and prayers
from the rest of the Society for Germany and the northern
countries suffering the ravages of the Reformation. Ignatius
took to the idea and immediately wrote a letter to the entire
Society requesting these prayers and stipulated that the
priests were to celebrate Mass once a month for this
intention, and that the nonpriests were to offer their prayers
for the same intention. Ignatius did not restrict this order to
European houses, but also asked the prayers of the brethren in
India. Though Canisius did not mention England by name,
Ignatius does so in his letter for news had recently arrived
that Mary Tudor succeeded to the English throne, and with a
Catholic queen now ruling England Ignatius hoped that that
nation would soon be brought back to the Catholic faith.
Since this letter was directed to all Jesuits, it was written in
Latin [Ep. 5:220-22].*

Jesus

Ignatius of Loyola, General of the Society of Jesus, to my beloved
brothers in Christ, superiors and subjects of the Society of Jesus,
everlasting health in our Lord.

The order of charity by which we should love the whole body

of the Church in her head, Jesus Christ, requires a remedy to be applied, especially to that part which is more seriously and dangerously affected. Therefore, it seems to us that we should, as far as our slender resources allow, bestow with special affection the help the Society is able to give to Germany and England and the northern nations which are so grievously afflicted with the disease of heresy.

Although many of us have already carefully attended to this by other means,[67] and applying Masses and prayers for many years now, still, in order to give this duty of charity a wider field and a longer life, we enjoin on all rectors and superiors, who are placed over others, to celebrate, if they are priests, and to have those under their authority celebrate one Mass each month to God; and those who are not priests, their prayers for the spiritual needs of Germany and England, so that at length the God of these nations and of all others that are infected with heresy may have pity on them and deign to lead them back to the purity of the Christian faith and religion.

It is our desire that these prayers continue as long as these nations need our help, and that no province, even those in farthest India, be exempt from this duty of charity.

From Rome, July 25, 1553.

23. TO FATHER NICHOLAS GOUDANUS

On the Gift of Tears

Rome,
November 22, 1553

Nicholas Goudanus[68] had been working in Germany and Austria alongside Peter Canisius since 1550. He was a selfless worker in the Lord's vineyard and, apparently, thought it would be good to have the gift of tears. Thus he wrote to Ignatius asking him to pray that that gift be granted him. In his response Ignatius, through his secretary Polanco, informs Goudanus that the gift of tears is not necessary for a fruitful

On the Gift of Tears

apostolate. To have a heart filled with compassion for the miseries of one's neighbor, and to seek to alleviate them are as pleasing to God as the gift of tears. Ignatius ends by encouraging him to keep his will strong and reminds him that this will be enough for his personal perfection. The language of the letter is Italian [Ep. 5:713-15].

The peace of Christ.

My dear father in Christ Jesus:

I received your letter of October 12, and it gives me great edification to see the desire you have of being of help to souls in Germany, not only by preaching and other external means, but also with your tears, which gift you desire from the giver of all good things.

As to the first of your desires, to be of definite help to the neighbor by the external means of preaching and so forth, we will beg of Christ unconditionally to deign to *give to his voice the voice of power* [Ps. 68:33], and to the administration of the sacraments the desired fruitfulness. But the gift of tears may not be requested unconditionally, nor is it, absolutely speaking, necessary and proper for all indiscriminately. However, I have taken the matter up with our Father Ignatius, and I myself have asked of God, and will continue to ask, that our Lord grant it to you in the measure that will be good for the end that your reverence has in seeking it, namely, the help of your own soul and the souls of your neighbor. *A hard heart shall fear evil at the last* [Sir. 3:26], but the heart, my dear father, that is full of the desire of helping souls, as is that of your reverence, cannot call itself hard in God's service. If in the will and the superior part of the soul, this heart feels compassion for the miseries of one's neighbor, and seeks to do what it can to relieve them and performs those services which a man of determined will undertakes, tears are not necessary for such a heart, nor other tenderness of heart.

Some indeed have tears naturally, when the higher emotion of the soul makes itself felt in the lower, or because God our Lord, seeing that it would be good for them, allows them to melt into tears. But this does not mean that they have greater charity or that they are more effective than others who enjoy no tears. They are no

85

less moved in the higher part of the soul—that is, in a strong and energetic will, which is the proper act of charity in God's service and the good of souls—than they who abound in tears.

I will tell you, reverend father, what I really think. And that is that, even if it were in my power to allow this gift of tears to some, I would not give it, because it would be no help to their charity, and would be harmful both to their heads and their health and, consequently, stand in the way of every act of charity. Do not lose heart, then, because of this absence of external tears, but keep your will strong and energetic, and manifest it in your actions. This will be sufficient for your own personal perfection, the help of others, and the service of God. Remember that the good angels do what they can to preserve men from sin and obtain God's honor. But they do not lose courage when men fail. Our father has much praise for those of Ours who in this sense imitate the example of the angels. No more for the present, except to commend myself to your reverence's prayers.

From Rome, November 22, 1553.

24. TO FATHER PHILIP LEERNUS

A Letter of Encouragement

Rome, December 30, 1553

The college in Modena opened in 1552, and Philip Leernus[69] was its second rector. He wrote to Ignatius protesting his unsuitableness to the task especially because of the dryness of soul he was then experiencing. In this letter of encouragement, Ignatius exhorts him to have confidence in God and in His divine gifts. What is important is solid virtue, and spiritual relish does not make a man perfect nor is it necessary in the divine service. The letter was written in Italian [Ep. 6:109-10].

The peace of Christ.

My dear Father Master Philip:

The office of rector which your reverence holds is in good hands. You ought to be on your guard that your desire for humiliation does not yield to the spirit of faintheartedness. We should not have a petty regard for God's gifts, though we may and should despise our own imperfections. Let your reverence be of good heart and let your companion, Master Giovanni Lorenzo,[70] help you when he can. Do not lose heart or belittle yourself. Be assured that we have a higher esteem of God's gifts in your reverence than you yourself have.

As to that blindness or dryness of soul which you think you find in yourself, it may easily come from a lack of confidence, or faintheartedness and, consequently, can be cured by the contrary. Above all remember that God looks for solid virtues in us, such as patience, humility, obedience, abnegation of our own will—that is, the good will to serve Him and our neighbor in Him. His providence allows us other devotions only insofar as He sees that they are useful to us. But since they are not essential, they do not make a man perfect when they abound, nor do they make him imperfect when they are absent.

I will say no more, except to pray that Jesus Christ our Lord may be our strength and the support of us all.

From Rome, December 30, 1553.

25. TO TEUTONIO DA BRAGANÇA

On Sickness as   Rome,
an Exercise of Virtue   January 1, 1554

Teutonio da Bragança[71] was a young Jesuit who, despite his illness, wanted to study in Rome. Ignatius wrote to him exhorting him to reap spiritual fruit from his illness and

87

suggests that, because of his health, he not come to Rome but go to Córdoba to continue his studies. The letter was written in Spanish [Ep. 6:130-31].

May the sovereign grace and everlasting love of Christ our Lord be always our strength and support.

Letters from Master Nadal, our commissary, inform me, my dear brother, that God our Lord has afflicted you with no slight illness. I am quite convinced in His Divine Goodness that this illness has been sent you in the interest of more important health, as an occasion for merit and the exercise of virtue. I am sure that you have tried to draw the fruit which God our Lord wishes you to draw from such visitations. In His infinite mercy and love He seeks our greater good and perfection no less with bitter medicines than with consolations that are sweet to the taste. Nevertheless, I hope with His divine favor soon to have news of your improvement, and I am sure that you will make much use of your better health in His service.

As to your coming to Rome, though it would give us the greatest consolation to see you, yet considering that in all this time there has been no opportunity to satisfy this desire which we both have, I suppose that we had better, taking your illness into account, give that thought up for the present, and that it would be more for your progress in studies and your spiritual consolation if you were to go to Córdoba where you will be able to continue your education. Put aside whatever other cares you may have, and rest assured that we will look after you, and that in the end all will be for the greater service and glory of our Lord. May His Infinite and Supreme Goodness grant us all the bountiful grace to know and do His most holy will.

From Rome, January 1, 1554.

26. TO FATHER JERÓNIMO DOMÉNECH

On Preferring the Universal Good of the Society over that of a Particular Province

Rome, January 13, 1554

Jerónimo Doménech[72] was provincial of Sicily and was concerned about the lack of Jesuits to staff the various positions in his province. He wrote to Ignatius complaining of the few men who had been sent him for a harvest so vast, and had commented to some that the founder was not sending men to Sicily because he had little interest in the place. Ignatius heard of this remark and directed Polanco to write this letter of reproof. Polanco writes that Ignatius did not appreciate the provincial's comment, informs him that the other houses in Italy are likewise suffering from lack of men, and reminds him that Ignatius has to consider the universal good of the Society rather than that of any single province. By enumerating the several Italian colleges that were understaffed, Polanco shows that Sicily is the best provided of all. Doménech is, of course, to make his needs known to Ignatius, but he is then to leave everything in the general's hands. Polanco's letter was written in Spanish [Ep. 6:178-80].

The peace of Christ.

My dear father in Christ:

I would much prefer to write in a way that would console you rather than offend you, but your reverence must refrain from giving occasion. Indeed, if our father were not kept busy by other pressing matters, he would show in a much more effective manner his dislike of your reverence's complaints, which reflect discredit on him, not only because you do not submit your own judgment to his in his appointments but because, in the presence of others, you also condemn them as being bad. This is clearly seen in the instance of the three who had recently come from Spain.[73] You tried to keep Master Pierre Chanal,[74] and you complained to him that, while our father in the beginning sent you outstanding men of the Society, he later withdrew all of them, and so forth.

Your reverence overlooks the fact that some recompense had been made for those who were taken away, and you fail to see (something still more surprising) that our father is obliged to keep the universal good in mind. Thus, besides providing you with enough men to carry on the works you have undertaken, he must assist others in places where our Lord wishes to make use of the Society and its members. The college of Venice has only one priest,[75] who has no knowledge of philosophy or theology; that of Padua has two[76] who are weak in literature and without advanced training; that of Modena has two[77] who are only average in Latin and still mere youths. At Ferrara, Pelletier[78] was alone until another was sent to help him, who does not know a great deal of literature or higher studies.[79] Father Francesco Palmio[80] is at Bologna, but no other priest can be sent as companion to him, since there is no other. Master Louis[81] is at Florence, and another[82] who has only with difficulty completed his literary studies. There are two at Gubbio,[83] but neither of them is a theologian. There is a single theologian at Perugia[84] and another[85] who is no theologian. And I think that there is an equal or even greater lack of schoolmasters in these places. But this does not prevent them from producing fruit, God making up for what our poor efforts cannot accomplish. If we compare conditions in Sicily with conditions in all of Italy, there is no doubt that it is better provided than any other place, even after making all necessary allowances.

Now, despite all this, our father does not wish that your reverence fail to declare your mind. Rather it is his wish that you do so, but he does not wish that your reverence allow any word to escape that would seem to indicate that you are complaining of what he does. Do not broadcast your needs abroad. He will be content if you make them known to him, and then leave everything to him. You should prefer the general good to the particular, and convince yourself that our father, once he has been informed simply, and without any attempt to use pressure, will decide what will be to the greater service of God our Lord and the general good. Indeed, this should be the aim of all, even though local angels have a special preference for their particular provinces or localities.

To help your reverence not to forget to keep confidential what you think you need in Sicily, and to write by way of representation and so forth, send in your own writing what you think of doing. This our father expressly commands. Try also to console him occasionally, seeing that he has so much trouble keeping so many places here in Europe and in Ethiopia supplied with men, besides maintaining this university in Rome, where there is much sickness among the professors and students. Doctor Olave,[86] who lectured twice a day in theology, is worn out, and it has become necessary to relieve him of one course to preserve his health. This course will be taken over by Master Jean,[87] who has just come from Sicily. However, God is our help, whose glory we seek in Sicily, Rome, and everywhere.

May He fill us with knowledge of Him and hope in Him, and dwell in our souls with perfect love. Amen.

From Rome, January 13, 1554.

27. TO FATHER GASPAR BERZE

On Moderation
in Penance

Rome,
February 24, 1554

Gaspar Berze[88] *was a remarkable missionary in India who, never thinking of himself, wore himself out for the good of souls. In April 1552 Francis Xavier appointed him rector of Saint Paul's College in Goa, and vice-provincial. Having heard that Berze's health was far from what it should have been, Ignatius wanted to rein in that excessive zeal of his and, thus, he directed Polanco to compose this letter, instructing Berze to moderate his penances, and in the matter of his health to place himself under the care of someone of his own choosing. In addition, since the Europeans were greatly interested in learning about exotic lands, Ignatius asks him to write about*

India—the land, and its flora and fauna. Unknown to Ignatius, however, as this letter was being drafted, Berze had been dead four months. While preaching Berze suffered an attack and had to be carried from the pulpit; he lingered for twelve days and then died on October 18, 1553. He literally worked himself to death in the vineyard of the Lord. Polanco composed this letter in Spanish [Ep. 6:357-59].

The peace of Christ.

My dear father in Jesus Christ:

May the grace and peace of Christ our Lord be present in ever-growing measure in our souls.

I did not think that we would be writing more than we have already done for this sailing,[89] but we only recently received a letter from Portugal, written in Goa, concerning your reverence's illness, and the work you continue to do in spite of it, preaching and so forth. Our father has thought it best to write this letter to your reverence, to inform you, as coming from him, that such action on your part does not seem wise, nor is it something that can long endure. Though he is much edified by your holy zeal and love of mortification, he does not think that it is seasoned with that salt which God our Lord looks for in every sacrifice, namely, a *reasonable service* [Rom. 12:1], such as Saint Paul wishes to see in those who offer themselves to God our Lord.

There are two drawbacks in dealing with yourself so severely. The first is that without a miracle your reverence will not last long in the holy ministries you undertake; rather, death will tie your hands. Or you will become so ill that you will no longer be able to continue them, which would be to put quite an obstacle in the way of God's service and the help of souls, in which works you could, with better health, employ yourself for many years to come. The second is that, being so harsh with yourself, you could easily come to be excessively so with those under your charge. And even though you give them no more than your example, it must result in making some of them run too fast, and especially so among the better of your subjects.

In a word, our father recommends moderation to your reverence. He would not have you preach when you are ill unless your physician says that such exercise will do you no harm. Since in your own cause your reverence might doubt just where moderation should begin, it would be good to choose someone who is living with you in Goa, or someone who accompanies you, who should have authority over you in the matter of food, sleep, and the amount of work to be undertaken. You should obey him in the Lord on all these points. We have made use of such means here in order to control the activity of some of the outstanding men of the Society and who hold important positions in it. This should suffice for the care of your person.

Some important people in the city, who read with great profit to themselves the letters from India, usually wish, and on various occasions have asked, for something to be written about the general cosmography of the countries to which Ours are sent. They would like to know, for instance, the length of the days in summer and winter, when summer begins, whether the shadow falls to the left or to the right. In a word, they would like information about anything that appears extraordinary, such as unknown animals and plants, their size, and so on. And this sauce for the taste of a certain innocent curiosity in man can be sent in the letters themselves, or on separate sheets.

And since we have observed in persons of quality and understanding that this exerts a very good influence on them, it will be good if, in the letters which can be shown to those outside the Society, less time is spent on those things which concern members of the Society and more given to matters of general interest. Otherwise the letters cannot be printed here without considerable editing. It is true that what concerns members of the Society will have more edification for our own members here; but this can be taken care of separately. If in the latter case they miss the mark, some remedy can be applied here, though it will cause some inconvenience. But the former cannot be supplied by us here. Your reverence can see to it that the members of the province write as directed.

For other matters I refer you to the other letters, and I will say no more here than that in this house, the Roman College, and the German College, we are all well by God's grace. May Jesus Christ our God and Lord, who is the health and true life of the world, give us the health and life that is interior. Amen.

From Rome, February 24, 1554.

28. TO FRANCESCO DE ATTINO

On Preserving One's Health
for God's Service

Rome,
April 7, 1554

Francesco de Attino[90] was a scholastic teaching in Sicily and because of a touch of pulmonary tuberculosis was told by his physician to return to his native air to recuperate. Being still young he wanted to stay with his Jesuit brethren in Naples and enjoy the consolation of their company, rather than living at home with his family. Thus he wrote to Ignatius asking to remain in Naples. But Alfonso Salmerón, who was then superior in Naples, not waiting for Ignatius's letter to arrive, ordered the youth to return to Atina to recover his health. Ignatius's letter is full of affection and concern for the young scholastic, and tells him that for the present it is better for him to forgo the consolation of living with his Jesuit brethren so that he could regain his health. Ignatius assures him that though he may be temporarily living outside the Society, nevertheless, he still remains a member because all Jesuits are bound in spirit. This letter was written in Italian [Ep. 6:585-87].

May the grace and peace of Christ always abide and grow in our souls.

Beloved brother in Christ Jesus, Master Francesco:

You will have understood the answer to your letter if you have remained in Naples. Our father desires every spiritual consolation for you. Because you would find consolation among your spiritual brothers and fathers in Naples, he gave you permission to remain there if your health could endure it. But since the physician thought that you should by all means seek your native air to restore your health, this benefit should be preferred to consolation.

Be certain of this, my dear brother, that, though you are separated from us in body, we feel that we are intimately united in the bond of charity, and that you feel the same way. But you must be sure of being united, not only by this bond, but also by that of holy obedience, which binds all the members of our Society into one spiritual body, to which you will belong no matter where you are. Remember that it is through obedience that you are making use of all these remedies and cures and every form of acceptable recreation, even physical, that is suggested to you. Because all the sooner, then, with God's help you will be freed from your illness to give yourself entirely to the service of God.

And do not think that trying to recover your health is an easy task. Your only purpose in desiring it is to serve God, and according to His holy will. Even though you use every reasonable means to get well, great resignation is required if you are to be content with whatever disposition God makes of you. As long as He visits you with illness, accept it from His hand as a very precious gift from the wisest and most affectionate of fathers and physicians. Be resolved especially both in mind and body, in work and in suffering, to be content with whatever pleases His Divine Providence. And write once in a while at least, even though it be but a few lines.

Master Pompilio[91] tells me that you have asked for some spiritual books. It would be good for you to read from time to time or have someone read to you, for your soul's refreshment and consolation, but do not spend much time in reading or in many devotions, especially those that require mental activity, as this would be to close the door on your recovery, which is the very reason for your going home and for the obedience that sent you. Use moderation, therefore, in every mental exercise. Remember that bodily exercise, when it is well ordered, as I have said, is also prayer by means of which you can please God our Lord.

May His grace be ever abundant in your soul. We all earnestly commend ourselves to your charity.

From Rome, April 7, 1554.

29. TO FATHER PETER CANISIUS

On the Society's Duty to Oppose Heresy

Rome,
August 13, 1554

During the late spring of 1554, Ferdinand I, King of the Romans, wrote to Ignatius telling him of the mayhem that Protestant catechisms and epitomes of theology were doing in his lands, and he urged on Ignatius the need of providing a theological manual that could serve for the instruction of theological students, university students, and country priests who needed help in preparing their weekly sermons. As early as 1550 Peter Canisius saw the need for such a compendium; Claude Jay began to prepare one but his death in August 1552 ended the project. This compendium had been envisaged as a text to replace the Sentences of Peter Lombard, but Canisius felt there was a greater and more immediate need, namely, a catechism to be placed in the hands of the students of college and high-school age, as well as in those of children. Thus he turned his full attention to this task, and by the time the instruction below was sent to him, he had already completed the first draft of his catechism.

In his instruction, Ignatius lists several ways that the Society could fulfill its obligation to stop the spread of Protestantism in northern Europe. He suggests that the Jesuits prepare a textbook for an abbreviated theology course for the less capable students, a catechism for children, and pamphlets that could easily be distributed among the faithful. Also, their students, if capable, could go into the suburbs and teach Christian doctrine, and finally the Society could open more colleges and schools. By the end of 1554, Canisius's catechism was at the press and it finally appeared in March 1555 with the title Summary of Christian Doctrine. It was intended for college students. Canisius then translated it into German in 1556 and worked on an adaptation for secondary-school students, which he called Shorter Catechism, and finally a version for younger children which he called

Catholic Catechism. *Canisius's catechisms immediately gained general acceptance; they went through countless editions during the author's own lifetime. This instruction was written in Italian [Ep. 12:259–62].*

JHS

Seeing the progress that the heretics have made in so short a time, spreading the poison of their evil teaching throughout so many countries and peoples, and making use of the verse of the Apostle to describe their progress, *and their speech will eat its way like gangrene* [2 Tim. 2:17], it would seem that our Society, having been accepted by Divine Providence among the efficacious means to repair such great damage, should not only be solicitous in preparing the proper remedies but should be ready to apply them, exerting itself to the utmost of its powers to preserve what is still sound and to restore what has fallen sick of the plague of heresy, especially in the northern countries.

The heretics have made their false theology popular and presented it in a way that is within the capacity of the common people. They preach it to the people and teach it in the schools, and scatter pamphlets that can be bought and understood by many; they influence people by their writings when they cannot reach them by preaching. Their success is largely due to the negligence of those who should have shown some interest; and the bad example and the ignorance of Catholics, especially the clergy, have made such ravages in the vineyard of the Lord. Hence it would seem that our Society should use the following means to end and cure the evils which the Church has suffered through these heretics.

In the first place, sound theology, which is taught in the universities and must have its foundation in philosophy and which requires a long time to acquire, is adapted only to alert and agile minds; because the weaker ones, who lack a proper foundation, can become confused and collapse, it would be good to prepare a summary of theology dealing briefly with topics that are essential but not controversial. In matters controversial there could be more detail, but it should be accommodated to the present needs of the people. It should solidly prove dogmas with appropriate arguments from Scripture, tradition, the councils, doctors, and refute the contrary teaching. It would not require too much time to teach such theology, since it would not go very deeply into other matters. In this way, many theologians could be prepared in a short time, who could attend to preaching and teaching in various places. The abler students could be given advanced courses which include greater detail. Those who do not succeed in these advanced courses should be removed from them and placed in the shorter course of theology.

The principal conclusions of this theology could be taught to children from a short catechism, as Christian doctrine is now taught, and also to the common people who are not yet too corrupted by heresy and are incapable of subtleties. This could also be done with the younger students in the lower classes, where they could learn it by heart.

It would be good to teach, at an hour of the day when they are not attending lectures, the above-mentioned summary of theology to students in the higher classes, such as the first and perhaps the second, and those in philosophy and theology, so that all who have some aptitude will learn the *loci communes*, and will be able to preach and teach Catholic doctrine, and refute the contrary, at least sufficiently enough to satisfy the needs of the people. This would seem to be especially the case in the colleges of upper and lower Germany and in France, and in other places where there is the same need. As for those who have no talent for serious study, or whose age will not permit it, it will be enough if, besides the study of languages, they attend the classes of this abridged theology course and the cases of conscience. They will thus become good and useful workers for the common good.

The local priests and the foreign students of the higher division, and any others so wishing, could be admitted to these theological classes; because of these classes it would not take long to provide many places with an antidote against the poison of heresy. Listening to the lectures with the textbook in their hands, they will be able to preach to the people and to teach in the schools what Catholic doctrine demands.

Another excellent means for helping the Church in this trial would be to increase the colleges and schools of the Society in many lands, especially where a good attendance could be expected.

There might possibly be need of a dispensation to accept colleges with fewer students than our Institute demands, or to begin classes without undertaking perpetual charge of a college, if indeed someone of Ours, or from elsewhere, can teach the said theology to the students and preach sound doctrine to the people; these measures, with the administration of the sacraments, will promote their spiritual welfare.

Not only in the places where we have a residence, but even in the surrounding neighborhood, our better students could be sent to teach Christian doctrine on Sundays and feast days. Even the extern students, should there be suitable individuals among them, could be sent by the rector for the same purpose. Thus, besides teaching correct doctrine, they will be giving the example of a good life, and by removing every appearance of greed they will be able to refute the strongest argument of the heretics—a bad life, namely, and the ignorance of the Catholic clergy.

The heretics write a good many pamphlets and booklets, by which they aim to remove all authority from the Catholics, and especially from the Society, and set up their false dogmas. It would seem imperative, therefore, that Ours also write answers in pamphlet form, short and well written, so that they can be produced without delay and purchased by many. In this way the harm done by the pamphlets of the heretics can be set aright and sound teaching spread. These works should be modest, but stimulating; they should point out the evil that is abroad and uncover the deceits and evil purposes of the adversaries. Many of these pamphlets could then be gathered into a single volume. Care should be taken, however, that this be carried out by learned men well grounded in theology, who will adapt the content to the capacity of the multitude.

With these measures it would seem that we could bring great relief to the Church, and in many places quickly apply a remedy at the outset of the evil and before the poison has had a chance to go so deep that it would be most difficult to remove it from the heart. We should use the same diligence in healing that the heretics use in infecting the people. We will have the advantage over them in that we possess a solidly founded, and therefore an enduring, doctrine. The most gifted students will then be able to follow a course of study in the Roman College and in other colleges of upper and lower Germany, as also in France. Later, when they are sent to different places where Ours have residences, they will become the directors and instructors of others.

30. TO THE WHOLE SOCIETY

On Dealing with   Rome,
Superiors   December 1, 1554

In December 1554 Ignatius drew up this instruction listing the norms to be kept when treating or dealing with superiors. He also gives rules regarding writing to Ours in distant places, and rules about the reception of candidates into the Society. Ignatius ordered that a copy of this instruction be sent to every Jesuit house, not only in Europe, but also in India, Brazil, and the Congo. This instruction exists in Spanish and Italian versions [Ep. 9:90-96].

Method of Treating and Dealing with Superiors

1. He who has business with a superior should have the matter well in hand, arranged in order, and thought out by himself or together with others, in keeping with the greater or lesser importance of the matter. In matters of lesser importance, however, or when there is need of haste and no time is available for study or consultation, it is left to his own judgment whether or not he should represent the matter to the superior.

2. After he has examined and studied his proposal, he should place it before the superior, and tell him that this matter has been examined by himself or with others, as the case may be. He should give the superior the results of his examination and study, but he should never say to a superior in discussing a point with him, "This or that is the right one," or "This is the way it should be," but he should speak conditionally and with a certain amount of reserve.

3. Once he has proposed the matter to the superior, it will be

the superior's duty to make a decision, or wait for further study, or refer the proposal back to him or to those who submitted it, or appoint others to examine it, or make the decision then and there, according to the nature of the difficulty involved.

4. If he points out some drawback in the superior's decision, and the superior should reaffirm his decision, there should be no answer or discussion for the time being.

5. But if, after the superior has made his decision, he who is dealing with him sees that something else would be better, let him call the superior's attention to it, giving his reason. And even if the superior has withheld judgment, this may be done after three or four hours, or a day. He could then represent to the superior what he thinks would be good, preserving, however, a manner of speaking and use of words that would neither be nor appear to be dissentient or quarrelsome. He should then accept in silence what is then and there decided.

6. But even supposing that a decisive answer had been given the first time, or even the second, he might, a month or more later, represent his view in the manner already indicated. For time and experience uncover many things, and the superior himself may change his mind.

7. He who deals with a superior should accommodate himself to the character and abilities of the superior. He should speak distinctly, so that he can be clearly heard, and whenever possible at an hour that is suited to the superior's convenience.

8. As far as possible, Ours should not wait until the day or the previous evening to write what should have been written by Saturday, or at other ordinary or extraordinary times when the post is about to leave for places beyond Italy, and then be forced to write in a hurry. But they should try to arrange to begin writing on the Sunday before what should be written by Saturday, and finish the dispatch by Wednesday evening, and leave as little as possible to be written in answer to letters received up to that time. In this way Thursday, Friday, and Saturday will be free to deal with and to answer other matters of importance that may turn up and need an immediate response.

9. Ordinarily do not write to different parts of Italy more than once a month; inform the rectors that this is in keeping with the orders given, unless something arises that does not permit a longer delay.

10. To places that are more distant, write every three months, unless something important happened, or the post is more frequent than usual.

11. Regarding the reception of candidates for the Society in Italy, the enclosed points[92] are sent to the colleges; these points deal with the qualities required in those who are to be admitted to the Society. And they should not receive anyone, or send anyone here, until we have been informed about them, point by point.

12. However, if there are some who impressively, and beyond the possibility of any doubt, fulfill the conditions set forth in the points, they may be received or even sent to Rome, if they are of such high standing, or if there be danger in delay, in which case superiors will have to use their own judgment. But it would be much better to advise the general in Rome and wait for an answer. There might be no difficulty about the candidates, but there might well be difficulty for the house in Rome.

13. We are sending these same points and directions everywhere; they had been prepared for Italy and Sicily (which is always to be understood when we speak of Italy). It will prove advantageous for other places to know what goes on in Italy, and these points may be of the greatest possible help to them. It is true that in places far distant from Rome, such as in other kingdoms, there is no need to consult with the general about admissions, or about sending men to Rome. But the charity and discretion of the commissary or provincial, with whom lower superiors such as rectors will consult, will take the place of consulting with the general. There could well be cases that will not allow the delay involved in consulting the general.

14. Provision has been made that a copy of this notice be sent to all places where there are any of the Society, and in the book in which this is entered in Rome a note has been made at the foot of the page indicating that it has been sent everywhere, and whether it has been received. Until such a time that a notice arrives of its receipt, let a reminder of this instruction be sent with each letter you write, and ask them to advise you of its receipt.

15. This same instruction is being sent to India, and the provincial there should send the same to the remote parts of his jurisdiction. The same dispatch can be sent from Portugal to Brazil and the Congo, although in such remote places, especially among

infidels and recently converted Christians, even though they should be helped by what is here written, it is left to the discretion of superiors, who, taking into consideration the condition of the region and other circumstances, will act according to their judgment about what is best for the greater glory of God and the greater spiritual progress of souls.

31. TO BARTOLOMEO ROMANO

On the Need for Interior Change

Rome, January 26, 1555

Bartolomeo[93] *was a scholastic at the college in Ferrara, and from various reports sent to Rome it appears that he was discontented, and complained about the school and the Jesuits in his community. Ignatius took no action until he had a chance to hear from Bartolomeo himself, and so he had Polanco write to him on November 24, 1554 [Ep. 8:96]. Bartolomeo answered Ignatius toward the end of December or early January, but his letter has not survived. From Ignatius's letter, however, we conclude that Bartolomeo was attributing his internal disquiet to his work at the college, his superiors, and those with whom he was living and, consequently, he requested a change of residence. In responding to him Ignatius tells him that it is his conduct that must change and not his place of residence. Bartolomeo's disquiet was coming from within him; unless that part of him changes, he will not be happy anywhere. Ignatius, therefore, exhorts him to practice humility, obedience, and self-denial. Finally, showing his interest in the young man, Ignatius asks him to write every month describing his progress in virtue and in studies. Ignatius's letter was written in Italian [Ep. 8:328–29].*

Jesus

The peace of Christ.

My dear Brother Bartolomeo:

From your letters and the letters of others, but especially from yours, we have some understanding of your state of mind. We are all the more disappointed in this, since we have such great desires of your spiritual good and eternal salvation.

You are mistaken in thinking that the cause of your disquiet, or little progress in the Lord, is due to the place, or your superiors, or your brethren. This disquiet comes from within and not from without. I mean from your lack of humility, obedience, prayer, and your slight mortification, in a word, your little fervor in advancing in the way of perfection. You could change residence, superiors, and brethren, but if you do not change the interior man, you will never do good. And you will everywhere be the same, unless you succeed in being humble, obedient, devout, and mortified in your self-love. This is the only change you should seek. I mean that you should try to change the interior man and lead him back like a servant of God.

Do not think of any mere external change, because if you are not good there in Ferrara, you will not be good in any college. We are all the more certain of this, for we know you can be helped more in Ferrara than elsewhere. I will give you one bit of advice: humble yourself sincerely before your superior, ask his help, open your heart to him in confession, or however you like, and accept with devotion the remedy he offers. Occupy yourself in beholding and bewailing your own imperfections rather than contemplating the imperfections of others. Try to give more edification in the future, and do not, I beg you, try the patience of those who love you in Jesus Christ our Lord, and who would like to see you His good and perfect servant.

Write me a few lines every month on how you are getting on with your humility, obedience, prayer, and the desire for perfection. Also let me know what progress you are making in your studies. May Christ our Lord have you in His blessing.

From Rome, January 26.

32. TO FATHER PONCE COGORDAN

Norms for Reforming Convents of Nuns

Rome, February 12, 1555

Ponce Cogordan[94] was treasurer in the Roman community where Ignatius lived. When Cardinal Marcello Cervini, the future Pope Marcellus II, was looking for someone to undertake the task of reforming a community of Benedictine nuns at the Monastery of Arta Cella in Auvergne, France, he chose Cogordan. Cogordan was not only equal to the task but, since he was a native of that part of France, he would know how to deal with the nuns and people, and would not appear to them as a total stranger. Cogordan's appointment came in December 1554, and he left Rome on February 13, 1555. Before his departure Ignatius prepared this instruction in which he explains the prudence and tact needed for Cogordan's mission. What Ignatius offers are broad principles and general norms, and these principles will serve to regulate this new ministry that was soon to become frequent in the Society. Ignatius composed this instruction in Spanish [Ep. 8:395–97].

Manner of Proceeding

1. Master Ponce should deliver the letters to those to whom they are addressed, and try to win the confidence of those who govern the province and to whom he is carrying letters, and he should have them write to the governor of the region and to several men of influence.

2. Deliver the letters to those of that region, and, as far as you can, cultivate their friendship, especially those who are relatives of the nuns.

3. Let everyone understand, both in public and in private, that you have come for the common good, and the honor of the monastery and of all that region. Deliver the bull of appointment and have it solemnly published.

4. Begin winning their confidence by conversing with men of high birth and others on spiritual matters, and by visiting the hospitals and other pious works, if there be any.

5. Visit the nuns showing them great kindness and make them understand that the cardinal sent you for their spiritual consolation. Give them the letter, but in the beginning do not speak of reform. You should first win their trust and that of the region too.

6. During this interval you should give them sermons and have exhortations in common, and speak on spiritual topics to individuals in private, and try to learn who are the more recollected and edifying. Win some of them over to our Lord, especially the abbess and other important nuns.

7. When you have made yourself acceptable to them, and come to know the hearts of the nuns, their former life, and their mistakes, begin your reform with tact. Learn who their confessor is; if he is one who cannot be of help, advise him to stay away for a definite time (and see to it that he does). But keep away from the nuns until you yourself have spoken to him. Try to win his friendship.

8. You should learn who the friar is and who the other persons are who frequent the monastery and with whom they speak. Advise them to stay away and see that they do. Do all you can to prevent all visiting, unless you know that some may help in obtaining the desired end. Use the help and support you may find in the nuns' relatives.

9. Persuade the nuns to remain enclosed for some time for their spiritual good, and keep everyone away from the monastery.

10. Get them especially to go to confession and Communion, and be particularly careful to get some of them to make a general confession, to gain the plenary indulgence and to be an example to others.

11. Help them with their examinations of conscience and with the Spiritual Exercises, especially at the beginning, with the exercises of the first week, and teach them methods of prayer that are suitable to each one.

12. Try with tact and charity to inspire them with confidence to open their hearts and reveal their defects, and give them to

understand in an unmistakable way that you are acting through charity and love and for their own good.

13. If some are hard to deal with, and are unwilling to cooperate, do not give up nor be annoyed with them. Show them rather a deep charity and a persevering wish to help them.

14. Do not resort to any coercive means with the nuns without fresh advice from us here at Rome.

15. Master Ponce is not to partake of the nuns' hospitality, nor is he to take anything by way of alms or in any other way.

16. Show no partiality, but manifest the same charity toward all.

Matters To Be Reformed

1. The nuns should observe enclosure, if possible, even though their institute does not oblige them to do so. Only rarely should they allow women, if they are of noble birth and of good name, to enter the monastery. But men, never.

2. They should lead a common life, and no one should have a servant or anything of her own.

3. They should recite the office in choir, and practice mental prayer and spiritual exercises.

4. They should confess and receive Communion every week, or every month, to a confessor of upright life and teaching—a man elderly in his ways as well as in his years. He should be appointed by the cardinal, or by the bishop with the approval of the cardinal.

5. Those who exercise authority in the region should each year choose two prominent women, elderly and upright, who will undertake to help the nuns in their needs, to see that they are living as they should, whether anyone open to suspicion visits them, and everything else that has to do with the monastery.

33. TO FATHER ROBERT CLAYSSON

On Avoiding an Overly Ornate Style

Rome,
March 13, 1555

Robert Claysson[95] was stationed in Paris and was a renowned and eloquent preacher. On December 1, 1554, following the instructions of his provincial, Paschase Broët, Claysson wrote the prescribed "quarterly letter"[96] to Rome. In reading it Ignatius found Claysson's style ample, inflated, and repetitious, and thus it became the occasion for the following letter. Ignatius indicates the style he would like used when writing to Rome, and recommends that it be modest and sober, and that there be a judicious selection of items. Ignatius's letter was written in Latin [Ep. 8:539–40].

The Peace of Christ.

Beloved in Christ, Master Robert:

In this letter from me you will recognize my affection for you, especially because I want to call your attention, without apology or excuse, to the style of your letter. While your letter is in some respects ornate and learned, we miss the proper decorum[97] in the ornament used and in the show of learning. It is one thing to be eloquent and charming in profane speech, and another when the one speaking is a religious. Just as in a matron an ornament that is modest and chaste is to be commended, so in the style which Ours should use when speaking or writing we do not look for what is self-indulgent and adolescent, but we look for a style that is dignified and mature. This is especially so in letters, where the writing, by its very nature, must be more compact and polished and manifest at the same time an abundance of ideas rather than an abundance of words.

Your charity will receive this admonition in good part, just as our charity did not permit us to let it go unnoticed. We do not dare send your letter anywhere without first making many changes in it.

Some selection of topics must also be made, and in the

quarterly letter only those items should be submitted which serve for edification. In many passages indeed there is a virile enough declaration of satisfaction in sharing the cross of Christ, but in some others the spirit seems weak and much less vigorous than one would expect in a soldier of Christ.

This, beloved brother, is our censure, and from it you will see that it is not only the Sorbonne that is allowed to exercise such a privilege.[98] In return for having written to you, as I think, with such frankness, confidence, and affection, I beg the reward of your prayers, and your admonition in turn, should occasion require it.

Yours in our Lord Jesus Christ.

Rome, March 13, 1555.

34. TO FATHER ALBERTO FERRARESE

On Hearing Women's Confessions

Rome, June 29, 1555

Alberto Ferrarese[99] had been in Venice but several months when he began to grow uneasy about the Venetian women coming to confession in dress that he considered immodest. Of the Jesuit priests in his community, he was the only one permitted to hear the confessions of women since the Inquisition there had stipulated that only priests who had reached their thirty-sixth birthday could serve as confessors for women. Ferrarese was, at this time, forty-five years old, and the only one in the community over thirty-six. Hence all women's confessions fell to him. In his letter Ignatius tells him how to deal with women who dress according to the Venetian fashion. Ignatius's letter was written in Italian [Ep. 9:266–67].

Jesus

The peace of Christ.

Beloved Father Master Alberto:

From father rector's letter we learn that your reverence is uneasy about the dress and personal adornment of the women of Venice, and you are quite right, for in this matter they frequently offend both God our Lord and are the cause of others offending Him. Where the practice is common, however, and there neither is, nor appears to be, any excess other than the said practice, and no intention of sinning or of causing others to sin, it is not considered mortally sinful. Moreover, if any women should do this to please her husband, there would not even be venial sin.

On other occasions we have written on this matter as follows. Where there is no notable curiosity—nothing beyond what is common—and no bad intention, though there might be some vanity in a woman so presenting herself as to display her charms, and so forth, they could be absolved the first time with an admonition and a bit of advice. But if they return and again confess this, especially if they are frequent communicants, you must make them give up this vanity and put an end to this bad practice, as much as possible. Should they be unwilling to comply, you could tell them that you will absolve them this time but not in the future, and if they do not wish to give up their vanity they should go to confession elsewhere. Even though you do not condemn them as guilty of mortal sin, there is great imperfection, and if one does not wish to give up such imperfection the Society will have nothing to do with them.

Your reverence may be allowing your zeal to mislead you, and so, in such cases, you should be guided by the judgment of the rector, since it is possible for him to know, outside of confession, what everyone knows and sees. Do not be timid or scrupulous when he thinks you should not be.

I will say no more, except that charity and the desire to help souls is accustomed to make the members of the Society brave, and in this way God helps them. I beg of Him to bestow upon your reverence the abundance of His grace.

From Rome, June 29, 1555.

35. TO ALL SUPERIORS OF THE SOCIETY

On Speaking the Language of the Country

Rome,
January 1, 1556

Ignatius insisted that Jesuits speak the language of the country where they reside, and he saw this as an indispensable means of promoting unity in the community. At the beginning of each year this instruction was renewed and sent to all superiors, and eventually was incorporated into the Common Rules (#10). To help the non-Italian Jesuits in Rome, Ignatius arranged for Italian classes three times a week, but then in 1555 he changed it to daily classes. This instruction exists in an Italian version [Ep. 10:451–52].

Jhus

The Peace of Christ.

It seems fitting for the benefit and edification of the peoples among whom our Society is living, and for the increase of union, charity, and good will among Ours, that in places where we have a college or a house all who do not know the language which is in common use should learn it and as a rule speak it. If each one were to speak his mother tongue, there would be much confusion and lack of union, seeing that we are of different nations.

For this reason our father has given orders that in all places where the Society exists, all of Ours should speak the language of that country. In Spain, Spanish; in France, French; in Germany, German; in Italy, Italian; and so on. He has given orders that here in Rome all should speak Italian, and every day there are lessons in Italian grammar to help those learn it who are unable to use it. No one is allowed to speak to another except in Italian, unless it be to make clear the meaning of some words and thus be better understood. Once a week in the refectory, either at dinner or supper, there is an Italian sermon in addition to the tones which is regularly held. Care is taken that some of those who are skilled in Italian help the others, so that they can compose their sermons with greater ease. A good penance is given to those who fail in their observance of this regulation.

Likewise our father has given orders that this same rule be written out and kept everywhere in the Society as carefully as possible, due consideration being had for differences of places and persons. For this reason we are writing to your reverence to see that the regulation is observed. Please advise us when you receive this.

May Jesus Christ be with us all.

From Rome, January 1, 1556.

36. TO FATHER ADRIAN ADRIAENSSENS

On Frugality in Meals
Rome,
May 12, 1556

Adrian Adriaenssens[100] was rector of the college in Louvain. Since that community was composed of people of different nations, who were accustomed to different types of food, Adriaenssens wrote to Ignatius, in a letter no longer extant, to ask his opinion on the quality of the meals that should be served in the community. Ignatius proposes that the meals be frugal, and that the food served be that which is ordinary in that locale and easily obtainable. While Ignatius writes this for those who enjoy good health, at the same time he insists that those who are ill should receive all that they need, and any extras that the physician may prescribe for them. That Ignatius is emphatic with regard to special treatment for the sick, may indicate that the rector might have been a bit too strict with them.[101] Ignatius's letter was written in Latin [Ep. 11:374–75].

Jhus

The peace of Christ.

We have received your reverence's letter dated the last of March, and to answer all your points briefly, I praise your thriftiness and economy and your doing your best to give a good example in all that concerns food. I do not think it is good, however, to withhold what the physician thinks is necessary for the recovery or the preservation of health, though he too ought to keep our poverty in mind. This much in general. It is good, moreover, to get accustomed to the more common and more easily obtainable food and drink, especially if one enjoys good health, and it is quite in keeping with reason and our Institute, which directs that Ours make use of those foods that are common and ordinary.

Therefore, if health permits, one should get accustomed to beer, or even water, or cider, where this drink is in common use, and not make use of imported wines, at greater expense and with less edification. Some among you, however, may be in ill health, such as Master Adrian Witte,[102] Master Bernard,[103] and Master Pedro de Ribadeneira.[104] If one takes proper care of his body he will have enough strength for works of zeal and charity, and for the help and edification of his neighbor. If he does not do so, he will grow weak and feeble, and will be of little advantage to the neighbor. He will then have to receive care, as has happened to Master Bernard and Master Adrian when they were in Italy. I would by no means make these men get used to a coarser diet unless it could be done without injury to their health. Rather, I would prefer that God's servants, and all those who are ready for heavy labors for Christ, have these comforts than to see others enjoy them who are less useful for the common good.

Care should also be taken that what is merely superfluous should not be allowed to slip in under the guise of necessity, and things that merely cater to the senses as conducive to health, thus turning a praiseworthy practice into an abuse. Should it be contrary to edification to take some of these extras in public, as those foods that have been ordered by the physician as necessary, see that they are then taken in private. In a word, all that is needed for health should be provided, but without scandal. This is what may be said in general, and prudence will make the application in particular cases. Decide what is to be done in each case after weighing all the circumstances.

May our Lord give us the light of holy discretion to make use of creatures in the light of the Creator.

Rome, May 12, 1556.

Spiritual men will not think it strange or reprehensible to have different food and drink on the same table to answer the needs of those in good or in poor health. But to avoid scandalizing those who are weaker, should there be any present, these special foods can be taken at other times. We must not forget Paul's warning against scandalizing the weak.[105]

37. TO BROTHER GIOVANNI BATTISTA

On the Desire to Study

Rome,
May 23, 1556

Brother Giovanni Battista[106] was the buyer at the Jesuit college in Padua and for some time had been growing unhappy as a coadjutor brother and now desired to take up studies. He made this proposal to his rector, who in turn passed it on to Ignatius in Rome. Ignatius interpreted the brother's desire for studies to be a temptation of the devil, and within that framework he wrote to him telling him that he is surprised that the brother had fallen for the devil's ruse. Ignatius adds that considering Giovanni's age and his natural capabilities, studies would be a waste of time, and reminds him that in the Society, as in the human body, there is a variety of members, and that each member must be content with the task that God offers him through the will of the superior. Finally, Ignatius ends saying that one needs obedience and resignation to remain a true religious. Ignatius's letter is in Italian [Ep. 11:437–38].

114

Jesus

The peace of Christ.

My dear Brother Giovanni Battista:

We are not surprised at your temptation regarding studies, for we know that it is the devil's work to annoy and disturb the servants of God. But you should be surprised at yourself for having yielded to it, forgetting that a religious should have no will of his own, and that he may do God's will he should follow the will of his superiors. And you have all the less reason for yielding to the devil's suggestion in this matter, since you were expressly told from the very beginning not to think of studies, but to exercise yourself in the offices of charity and humility. Taking into account your age and your aptitudes, it was thought that you would be wasting your time in study, and that you could make better use of it in other employments in God's service.

In the body all the members are not eyes, nor ears, nor hands, nor feet. And as each member has its function, and is satisfied with it, so likewise in the body of the Society all cannot be learned, nor all priests, but each one must be content with the employment given him according to the will and judgment of the superior, who will have to give an account to God for all his subjects.

Finally, Giovanni Battista, if you have given all to God, allow yourself to be guided by God, and act not in your own way, but in God's way. And you will have to learn this by obedience to your superior.

If someone tells you something different, even though he is transformed into an angel of light, be sure that he is the devil who is trying to draw you out of the Society. The Society will not put up with this self-will of yours if you do not really amend. You may have the name of religious, but if you fail in obedience, you are not a religious at all. Now, for the good we desire for you, we want you to examine yourself and to get over the way of acting you have had in this matter for some time now.

May God our Lord grant you His grace.

From Rome, May 23, 1556.

38. TO EMERIO DE BONIS

On Preserving Chastity   Rome,
                                    May 23, 1556

Emerio de Bonis[107] was a scholastic teaching in Padua, had been in the Society only five years, and felt somewhat insecure in it. He had been suffering temptations against chastity and decided to write to Ignatius, in a letter that has not survived, opening his soul to him and manifesting his troubled spiritual state. Ignatius had Polanco write a most consoling letter to him, indicating remedies he might put to use. Ignatius also offers him the opportunity of coming to Rome to continue his studies. Later in life de Bonis became an eminent director of souls and spiritual writer. Polanco wrote this letter in Italian [Ep. 11:439-40].

Jhus

The peace of Christ.

My dear Master Emerio in Christ:

Our father has understood what you wrote. Though you show great courage in overcoming the enemy who up to the present has harassed you, but by God's grace has not overcome you, he leaves it to you to decide, judging that it would be to your greater consolation, whether to come to Rome next September, or to remain in Padua, or to change to some other college in which you could take charge of the first class, as you do there.

In this way you will, with God's help defend yourself. Besides your prayer, make it a point not to look at anyone fixedly in the face, which might cause you any uneasiness of heart. In general, when you deal with the neighbor, let your eyes be averted, and try not to think of this one or that one as handsome or ugly, but rather as the image of the most holy Trinity, as a member of Christ and bathed in His blood. Moreover, do not become familiar with anyone. It will be enough if, in school, you fulfill your task as teacher in pure charity and obedience. Always deal with your students in public and not in private, and extern students should not be allowed the run of the house, unless the rector has, in some particular case, given permission. By attending to your progress in God's service and the way of perfection, God will continue to help you.

Also be on your guard against those times and occasions when you are usually attacked. Briefly raise your mind to God. And above all, make a real effort to abide in His presence, frequently recalling that His Infinite Wisdom is present both to the inner and exterior man.

There is no need to multiply remedies if you make faithful use of these. And do not forget the first, which concerns the eyes. You will, then, never complain with him who says: *my eyes cause me grief* [Lam. 3:51].

Our father and all of us commend ourselves in your prayers. From Rome, May 23, 1556.

39. TO FATHER JUAN MARIN

On Scruples

Rome,
June 24, 1556

Juan Marin[108] was a young Spanish Jesuit teaching in the Jesuit college in Bivona, Sicily. He did wonderful work among the people and manifested a great zeal for souls but, unfortunately, he had a scrupulous conscience and continually suffered torment therefrom. Ignatius was especially interested in him since he too had suffered from scruples and, thus, he wanted to do whatever he could to free Marin of his affliction. Ignatius, writing through Polanco, offers him remedies to overcome his scrupulosity, insisting that he must submit himself to the judgment of his superior and confide in God. Marin did not live to enjoy a scruple-free conscience, for only weeks after receiving Ignatius's letter he was suddenly taken ill and died on the following day, September 16. Polanco composed this letter in Spanish [Ep. 12:30–31].

Jhus

From the letters of Father Master Jerónimo[109] and also of Father Eleuthère,[110] our father has learned what God is pleased to accomplish through the ministry of Ours in your city. I am sure that He would make more use of them if your reverence's excessive scrupulosity, reinforced by the lack of humble resignation, had not proved an obstacle. Up to a certain point scruples are not harmful to the one suffering from them, when that person becomes, because of his scruples, more vigilant and careful about not offending God, and does not form a judgment that this or that is sinful, even though he has some doubt or fear that it is, and places his confidence in another person whom he should trust, setting aside his own judgment and accepting that of his adviser. If these two points do not help the scrupulous person, then he is in the gravest danger, not only of offending God by failing to avoid what he erroneously thinks is sin, but also of losing the opportunity and the ability to serve Him, and even his own good natural judgment.

So, Master Marin, determine to keep these two points fixed in your memory: (1) not to make any judgment or to decide by yourself that something is sinful when it is not clearly evident that it is and others do not think so; (2) when you fear that there is sin, you should refer the matter to the judgment of your superior, Father Eleuthère, and believe what he says, not because he is Master Eleuthère (even though he is a man of fine spirit and entirely trustworthy), but because he is your superior who holds the place of Christ our Lord. You should do the same with any other superior you may have: humble yourself and trust that Divine Providence will rule and guide you by means of your superior. And believe me, if you have true humility and submissiveness, your scruples will not cause you so much trouble. Pride is the fuel they feed on, and it is pride that places more reliance on one's own judgment and less on the judgment of others whom we trust.

Also beseech God in your prayers and Masses to free you from this suffering or infirmity, as far as is needful to avoid offending Him, or being an obstacle to His greater service, and ask the prayers of others for the same intention. Offering you mine, I commend myself to yours.

May Christ our Lord give us all His grace always to know and fulfill His most holy will.

From Rome, June 24, 1556.

40. TO FATHER FULVIO ANDROZZI

On the Exercises   Rome,
as an Efficacious Means   July 18, 1556
of Helping Souls

Fulvio Androzzi,[111] a Jesuit for less than a year, was carrying on an apostolate in Meldola, in the region of Emilia. He wrote two letters to Ignatius, which have not been preserved, informing him of the work he was doing, he was so busy, in fact, that he found that he had not sufficient time to prepare his sermons and asks Ignatius for direction. Through Polanco, Ignatius responds sending him various norms to be used in his apostolate. But Ignatius emphasizes that the most efficacious means of helping souls would be to give them the Spiritual Exercises. The first week for everyone, while the full four weeks only for a select few. He then adds that when there are many tasks to be done, one has to make a prudent selection to see which tasks take precedence over others. The letter was originally written in Italian [Ep. 12:141-43].

Jesus

The peace of Christ.

We have two letters from your reverence, one dated the twentieth of last month, and the other dated the fourth of this month. We rejoice in our Lord on the occasions which His goodness allows you to serve Him by helping and consoling souls, not only those of our benefactors but of their families and the people of their regions, and because of the health and peace of mind that He bestows on you. However, if little time is left for you to prepare your sermons, Christ our Lord will supply that defect. But throughout the day things might be so arranged as to give you more time, if more time is necessary, for one thing rather than for another. The good disposition and devotion of your patrons will be a great help to you in setting to order what should be better arranged. . . .

Your reverence knows that there is one outstanding means among those which of their nature are helpful to men. I mean the Exercises. I remind you, therefore, that you should make use of this weapon, which is such a familiar part of our Society. The first week could be given to many people, as well as some methods of prayer. But to give them exactly as they are, one should have retreatants capable and suitable for helping others after they themselves have been helped. Where this is not the case, they should not go beyond the first week. Your reverence should look about to see whether you can find some good prospects for the Lord's service, for whom there is no better way than the one I have indicated. The frequent reception of the sacraments is usually of much help to this end.

If you are very busy, you should make a choice and employ yourself in the more important occupations where there is greater service of God, greater spiritual advantage for the neighbor, and the more general or perfect good. Keeping a little time to put order in yourself and your activities will be of considerable help to you in this respect. . . .

With regard to your reverence's personal experiences, which you say are the cause of some pain and sadness, I hope that you will daily grow freer of them by God's grace, since all such things, and even the greater pains of our human nature, can be cured by greater enlightenment and an increase of charity. I hope that your reverence will find such a master in the Holy Spirit, who will make it less necessary on our part to multiply advice.

I am enclosing a letter from Ortensio,[112] and if you wish I will send you other letters which were sent us from Loreto. I understand that Curzio[113] is advancing with great strides along the way of virtue and edification. Master Giovanni Filippo[114] will write you about other matters.

May God grant us all His grace always to know and to do His will.

From Rome, July 18, 1556.

NOTES

1. Paschase Broët was born in Picardy in 1500. He studied at Amiens and was ordained in 1524. He spent the next ten years in a parish but then went to Paris in 1534. There he met Pierre Favre, made the Exercises, and pronounced his vows at Montmartre on August 15, 1536. As a Jesuit he labored in Siena (1537–40), and after his visit to Ireland (1541) labored in Italy (1542–51). He was provincial in France (1552–62) and died in Paris on September 14, 1562, while serving the plague stricken.

2. Alfonso Salmerón was born on September 6, 1515, in Toledo. He went to Alcalá to study and there met Diego Laínez. Together they went to Paris to find Ignatius. He was one of the original seven to pronounce vows at Montmartre on August 15, 1534. He served as papal theologian at the Council of Trent (1546, 1551, 1562) and was provincial of Naples from 1558–76. He died in Naples on February 13, 1585.

3. Francis Zapata was a Spanish priest working at the papal curia in Rome, and accompanied Broët and Salmerón on their trip to Ireland. He later entered the Society in 1546, but sometime in 1547 or early 1548 he was dismissed. He then entered the Franciscans and lived a life of virtue.

4. Giovanni Battista Viola was born about 1517, in the region of Parma, and entered the Jesuits as a priest in February 1540. He was sent to Paris as superior of the Jesuit scholastics studying there. He died in Milan on April 19, 1589.

5. Pierre Favre was born in Villaret, Savoy, on April 13, 1506, and in 1525 went to study at the University of Paris. There he met Ignatius and, having made the Exercises under his direction, joined him in his religious enterprise. He was ordained to the priesthood on May 30, 1534, and since he was the only priest among the first companions, it was he who celebrated the Mass in the crypt of Saint-Denis in Montmartre when Ignatius and group made their first vows on August 15, 1534. As a Jesuit Favre traveled widely, making the Society known in Italy, Germany, and Spain. He

returned to Rome and died there on August 1, 1546. On September 5, 1872, Pope Pius IX confirmed the devotion paid to him in his native land and by apostolic decree declared that Favre was among the blessed in heaven.

6. Diego Laínez was born in 1512 in Almazán, Spain. He attended the University of Alcalá, arriving there after Ignatius had left for Salamanca. In 1533 he went to Paris to meet Ignatius and was one of the original seven to pronounce vows at Montmartre on August 15, 1534. He likewise served as papal theologian during the conciliar sessions of 1551 and 1562. He was named provincial of Italy in 1552, made vicar general on the death of Ignatius in 1556, and was elected Ignatius's successor in 1558. He died on January 19, 1565.

7. See note 2 above.

8. See note 5 above.

9. Claude Jay was born between 1500–1504. As a youth he attended school with Favre in Savoy. He was ordained a priest and was conducting a small school when Favre visited him in 1533 and encouraged him to go to Paris to continue his studies. In Paris he made the Exercises under Favre's direction and pronounced his vows at Montmartre on August 15, 1535. As a Jesuit he worked in Italy (1537–41) and in Germany (1542–49). He attended the Council of Trent (1545–47) and the Diet of Augsburg (1550). He died in Vienna on August 6, 1552.

10. Simão Rodrigues was born in 1510 in the village of Vouzella in the diocese of Viseu in northern Portugal. He was first educated in Lisbon, then came to Paris in 1526 and studied at Collège de Sainte-Barbe with Ignatius. He is numbered among the first companions and he pronounced his vows at Montmartre on August 15, 1534. He was superior (1540–46) and provincial (1546–52) of the Portuguese province. In 1553 he was called to Italy where he remained until 1564 when he went to Spain. In 1573 he returned to Portugal and died at Lisbon on July 15, 1579.

11. Martín de Santa Cruz was born in Toledo and traveled to Rome to enter the Society in August 1541. He went to Portugal in April 1542 for studies, was ordained in 1544, and shortly thereafter was made rector of the college in Coimbra. He went to Rome in September 1547 to report on the state of the college and died there on October 27, 1548. His letter to Ignatius has not survived.

12. This letter may be found in *Ep. PP. Paschasii Broeti, Claudii Jaji, Joannis Coduri, et Simonis Rodericii (MHSI)* 547–53.

13. Ignatius is referring to *Ad fratres de monte Dei* lib. 1, c. 11, n. 32 (PL 184:328). This letter had been originally attributed to Saint Bernard, but since 1662 it has been ascribed to its rightful author, William of Saint-Thierry.

14. Plato mentions this as an inscription on the Temple of Apollo at Delphi (*Protagoras*, 343b).

15. *Ad fratres de monte Dei* lib. 1, c. 11, n. 32 (PL 184:328C).

16. *Ibid.*, lib. 1, c. 9. (PL 184:324).

17. *In Cantica* sermon 19, #7 (PL 183:866B).

18. Ribadeneira was born in Toledo on November 1, 1526. He went to Rome in 1539 as a page in the household of Cardinal Alessandro Farnese, and entered the Society on September 18, 1540. He first studied in Paris and Louvain, but in 1546 went to Padua. In 1549 he was assigned to teach in Palermo and remained in Sicily until 1552 when Ignatius called him to Rome to assist at the German College. He was ordained in 1553, and in 1555 went to Flanders to establish houses of the Society. He was provincial of Tuscany (1560–61), and of Sicily (1561–65), and visitor for Lombardy (1569–70). In 1567 Father General, Francisco de Borja, commissioned him to write Ignatius's biography, which appeared in Naples in 1572. He then went to Spain and remained there until his death in Madrid on September 22, 1611. Ribadeneira's letter may be found in *Ep. Mixtae (MHSI)* 5:649–50.

19. Juan Alfonso de Polanco was born in Burgos on December 24, 1517, and entered the Society in Rome in 1541. In 1542 he was sent to Padua for his studies, where he was ordained in 1546. He was called to Rome in early 1547 to be Ignatius's secretary, and held that position during Ignatius's lifetime, and also was the general's secretary for Diego Laínez and Francisco de Borja. He died in Rome on December 20, 1576.

20. See note 6 above.

21. See *Sermo in vig. Nat. Domini* (PL 183:89).

22. See *Sermo 345* (PL 39:1520).

23. Ovid, *De remedio amoris* v. 749.

24. Lucan, *Pharsalia* 1, 165.

25. See *Epistulae ad Lucilium* 80, 6.

26. Borja was born on October 28, 1510, the oldest son of the third Duke of Gandía. He married Eleanor de Castro of Portugal in 1529, and his cousin, Emperor Charles V, made him Marquis of Lombay in 1530, and named him Viceroy of Catalonia in 1539. Upon his father's death in December 1541, he succeeded to the duchy of Gandía. His first contact with a Jesuit was his meeting with Pierre Favre in 1542 or perhaps earlier. Having made the decision that he should enter the Society, which he did on October 9, 1546, he started a correspondence with Ignatius who permitted him to take his vows while still administering his estates. After receiving his doctorate in theology (August 1550), Borja went to visit Ignatius in Rome (October 1550–February 1551), and upon his return to Spain resigned his title in favor of his son Carlos and was ordained to the priesthood on May 23, 1551. Upon the death of Laínez, Borja was elected general of the Society on July 2, 1565. He died in Rome on September 30, 1572.

27. Johann Eck was a renowned German theologian, born in 1486. He came to Ingolstadt in 1510, and after Luther's break with

the Church entered into controversy with him and Karlstadt. Eck wrote many treatises against Luther, but his most famous work, *Enchiridion*, was directed against Melanchthon's *Loci communes*. He died in Ingolstadt on February 10, 1543.

28. See note 9 above.

29. Canisius, whose family name was Kanis, was born in Nijmegen, the Netherlands, on May 8, 1521. While studying in Cologne he heard about the recently established Society of Jesus and went to Mainz to search out Pierre Favre and to learn more about it. Favre led him through the Exercises and accepted him into the Society on May 8, 1543. He was ordained to the priesthood on June 12, 1546, and served as Cardinal Truchsess's *peritus* at the Council of Trent in 1547. His next assignment was teaching in Sicily, from which task he was called to go to Germany. Canisius remained at Ingolstadt until March 1552 when he went to Vienna, and then in 1555 to Prague. He was appointed provincial of Germany in 1556 and held that office until 1569, when he went to Innsbruck to spend his time writing. In 1580 he traveled to Fribourg, Switzerland, to establish a new college and remained there until his death on December 21, 1597. He was beatified by Pope Pius IX on November 20, 1864, and canonized by Pope Pius XI on May 31, 1925.

30. Such unhesitating obedience does not originate with Ignatius, but is part of the monastic tradition. In the fifth chapter of his Rule, Saint Benedict exhorts his monks to "lay down whatever they had in hand, leaving it unfinished."

31. This was Andrés de Oviedo. Born in Illescas, Spain, about 1517, he entered the Society in Rome in 1541. After his studies and ordination he was appointed (1545) rector of the Jesuit college at Gandía, and it was he who led Francisco de Borja through his novitiate training and received his vows on February 1, 1548. In 1550 Oviedo traveled to Rome with the duke and was present at the discussions on the Constitutions. He was made rector of the new college in Naples (1551), and later assigned to the mission in Ethiopia. He was ordained bishop on May 5, 1555, and became

Patriarch of Ethiopia on December 20, 1562. In Ethiopia he lived amid extreme poverty. He died in 1577.

32. See note 10 above.

33. Brandão did not long remain a Jesuit. After returning to Portugal he was assigned, in 1552, to go to the Portuguese mission in Africa. On his way to the port of Lisbon he decided that he really did not want to go to the Congo and so he abandoned the Society.

34. The tones was an exercise in declamation, a fixed formula meant to exemplify different emotions. The purpose of the exercise was to teach the young Jesuits the various modulations of voice necessary to carry a variety of emotions. It likewise indicated the type of gestures demanded by different types of oratory. The text of the tones, as used in the Roman College, may be found in *Regulae Societatis Iesu* (1540–1556) *(MHSI)* 254–55, note 9.

35. Araoz was born at Vergara, in the province of Guipúzcoa, in 1515, and went to Rome to make a way for himself in the world, but there he made the Exercises under Ignatius's direction and entered the Society in the spring of 1539. After his ordination in Rome (December 25, 1541), he was sent to Spain with Pierre Favre to make the Society known in that country. He became an eloquent preacher and for a time served as court preacher at Valladolid. In 1547 he became the first provincial of Spain, and in 1565 was appointed Spanish assistant. He died in Madrid on January 13, 1573.

36. This is a reference to Francisco de Borja and his son Juan. When Borja went to Rome toward the end of 1550, Juan traveled with him, and hence Ignatius got to know the son as well as the father. On their return to Spain, Araoz was in their party, and after a most tiring journey the group finally arrived in Oñate on April 7, 1551. At the end of that month Juan wrote to Polanco in Rome, informing him that both his father and Araoz were very tired and that they were eating practically nothing. And in his letter to Ignatius Juan wrote: "The duke and father provincial are treating themselves most poorly. They do not take care of their health, nor

do they allow others to do so. No one can tell them what to do with regard to food, sleep, prayer, and so on" (*Ep. Borgiae* [*MHSI*] 1:631). The duke and Juan remained at Oñate because the duke was waiting to hear from his cousin, the emperor, about his request to resign his title and, thus, unwilling to return to his estates in Gandía, Borja remained with Araoz in Oñate. The emperor finally granted his permission and shortly after Borja had renounced his title he was ordained to the priesthood (May 23, 1551). At the time that Ignatius wrote this letter he was unaware that the imperial permission had been granted and that Borja had been ordained a priest.

37. Pelletier was a Frenchman, who entered the Society in Paris in 1545. He came to Rome and was appointed (1551) the first rector of the Roman College. After several years in Ferrara, he returned to France (1559) and died at Toulouse on January 1, 1564.

38. See *Ep. Broeti* . . . (*MHSI*) 369-72.

39. Urban Weber (Textor) was bishop of Laibach (modern Ljubljana) and the king's confessor.

40. Godinho was born about 1520 near Evora, Portugal, and entered the Society in Lisbon on March 11, 1542. He died in Lisbon on September 4, 1569, caring for the plague stricken.

41. See note 26 above.

42. Miró was born in the province of Valencia in 1516, and entered the Society in Paris in 1541. He studied at Coimbra and was ordained there in 1544. He then taught in Gandía and was in Rome for the discussions on the Society's Constitutions in early 1551. He served as provincial of the Portuguese province (1552-56) and was Portuguese assistant (1564-73). He died in Rome on August 25, 1590.

43. Torres was born in the province of Aragon in 1507. He studied in Paris and became acquainted with Ignatius but always felt some antagonism toward him. Upon his return to Spain, Torres

taught at Alcalá and eventually became its rector. In 1542 he went to Rome on business for the university and again met Ignatius, made the Exercises, and decided to enter the Society. He secretly pronounced vows in 1545, and when his business was over in Rome he returned to Spain (end of 1546) and openly joined the Society's ranks in 1547. When it was time to open a Jesuit college in Salamanca, Torres was sent there as its rector (1548), and then on January 1, 1552, he was appointed visitor for Portugal. He became provincial of Baetica in 1554, and then succeeded Miró as provincial in Portugal in 1556. When his labors were completed in Portugal, he returned to Spain and died at Toledo during the night of October 23–24, 1593.

44. Leonard Kessel was born in Louvain about 1519 and there entered the Jesuits in December 1543. He was already a priest. He was sent to the Jesuit college in Cologne where he became rector of the community, spent his life, and died on October 26, 1574. The incident to which Ignatius refers took place in 1552 and his letter approving Kessel's action is dated October 4 of that year (*Ep.* 4:450).

45. See note 42 above.

46. Gonçalves da Câmara was a Portuguese born about 1519, and entered the Society in Lisbon on April 27, 1545. In 1553 he went to Rome to report on the state of the Portuguese province and remained there until October 1555, serving, in the meantime, as minister at the Jesuit residence. It was to Gonçalves da Câmara that Ignatius narrated his autobiography. He returned to Portugal but then on the election of Diego Laínez as the Society's second general, he was made Portuguese assistant. In 1559 he became tutor to the youthful King Sebastião, and died in Lisbon on March 15, 1575.

47. As early as 1546 João III had asked Ignatius to send missionaries to Ethiopia in order to bring the Abyssinian Christians back into the Church. Ignatius thought well of the plan and was willing to offer Jesuits for so noble an enterprise. While the king did nothing to further this plan for the next six years, Ignatius kept his interest in it and whenever the opportunity offered he reminded the king of the harvest waiting in Ethiopia. In this letter Ignatius

suggests that the king's confessor could prove a definite help in promoting the mission and in naming a patriarch. The king's interest did revive and in December 1553 he wrote to Ignatius requesting a dozen Jesuits for the mission. Those named as suitable to be patriarch were João Nuñes Barreto, Melchior Carneiro, and Andrés de Oviedo. The first was named patriarch and the other two were appointed his coadjutors. The bishops and missionaries left Portugal in March 1556, but of the three bishops only Oviedo (see note 31 above) reached Ethiopia.

48. See the eighteenth letter in this collection.

49. See note 46 above.

50. See *Ep. Mixtae (MHSI)* 3:31–40.

51. For a complete commentary on this letter, see Manuel Espinosa Pólit, *Perfect Obedience* (Westminster, Md.: Newman, 1947).

52. *Moralium* lib. 35, c. 14, n. 28 (PL 76:765B).

53. *Ibid.*

54. *Collationes* lib. 4, c. 20 (PL 49:608–9).

55. *Liber ad milites templi* c. 13 (PL 182:939A).

56. *Sermo 35, De tribus ordinibus ecclesiae* n. 4 (PL 183:636B).

57. *Collationes* lib. 2, c. 11 (PL 49:541B).

58. *Sermo 3, De circumcisione* n. 8 (PL 183:140C).

59. *Sermo 35, In Epiphaniae solem.* 5 c. 3 (PL 54:252A).

60. *Liber de praecepto et dispensatione* c. 9 (PL 182:871D).

61. *Sermo 89, De jejunio septimi mensis 4* c. 1 (PL 54:444B).

62. See *De Coenobiorum instit.* lib. 4, c. 24 (PL 49:183D–84B).

63. *Ibid.,* lib. 4, c. 26 (PL 49:186A).

64. See St. Gregory, *Vita Sancti Benedicti* c. 7 (PL 66:146A–B).

65. See *De vitis patrum* lib. 3, n. 27 (PL 73:755B–56B).

66. See note 29 above.

67. Among these means would have been the sending of Jesuits to Ingolstadt in 1549, to Vienna in 1551, and the opening of the German College in Rome in 1552.

68. Goudanus was a Dutchman, whose family name was Floris, but was known as Goudanus because he had been born in Gouda about 1517. He entered the Society as a priest in Louvain (1548), and then went to Rome. He was the first rector of the college in Venice and from there he went to Ingolstadt in 1550 and to Vienna in 1552. He attended the Conference at Worms in 1557, and when his health broke he went to recuperate at Louvain. In 1562 Pope Pius IV appointed him special papal envoy to visit Queen Mary Stuart in Scotland. He died at Louvain on November 10, 1565.

69. Leernus was born in Flanders, about 1525, in the small town of Leerneur, near Liège. His family name was Faber, but he was known in the Society as Philip Leernus, after his native town, as well as Philip of Flanders. He was already a priest when he entered the Jesuits in Rome in October 1550. He was first stationed at the college in Ferrara and became rector at Modena at the end of 1553. He died in Modena on February 26, 1558.

70. Giovanni Lorenzo Patarini was born on December 25, 1527, in Piacenza, and entered the Society on April 21, 1551. He studied at Bologna, was ordained there in March 1553, was then stationed in Ferrara, and moved to Modena with Philip Leernus. He died in Naples on November 7, 1557.

71. Bragança was born in 1530 of a noble Portuguese family and entered the Society on June 12, 1549. He was a great admirer of Simão Rodrigues, and when the latter was removed from office Bragança felt that Rodrigues had been harshly and unjustly treated. To help the young Jesuit achieve peace of soul, Ignatius again wrote to him in April 1554, permitting him to come to Rome. Bragança arrived in the Eternal City in October, but by the following September he left the Society. He eventually became archbishop of Evora, always remained friendly toward the Society, and died in 1602.

72. Doménech was born in Valencia in 1516, and was already a priest when he met Pierre Favre in Parma in 1539. He made the Exercises and was accepted into the Society in September of that year. He was rector of the students studying in Paris (1540-42), served as Ignatius's secretary in Rome (1544-45), was provincial of Sicily (1553-61, 1562-68, 1570-76), and rector of the Roman College (1568-70). He returned to Spain and died in Valencia on December 20, 1592.

73. The three priests were Pierre Chanal (see note 74 below), Jean Couvillon (see note 87 below), and Jean de la Goutte. They sailed from Spain in late 1553, and landed in Sicily and then made their way toward Rome. De la Goutte, known as Guttanus, was, unfortunately, captured on his way to Rome by Turkish pirates somewhere near Naples, and all attempts to secure his release proved fruitless. He died in 1555. The other two arrived in Rome shortly before this letter was written.

74. Pierre Chanal, known as Canal or Canale, was born near Lyons, about 1526. He entered the Jesuits in Paris (1543), studied in Spain, and was recalled to Rome to teach at the Roman College. He died at Billom in 1562.

75. This was Cesare Helmi, rector of the college. He was born in Foligno in 1522, entered the Jesuits in Rome (1549), and died in Venice on July 31, 1576.

76. The two in Padua were Giovanni Battista Tavona and Luigi Nappi. The former was rector of the college, having been born in Modena about 1520. He entered in Rome (1541), and died in Bivona on September 21, 1573. Nappi was born in Milan, about 1531, entered in Rome (1550), was ordained priest in Padua (1553), and died in Milan on July 22, 1589.

77. Those in Modena were Philip Leernus (see note 69 above), and Giovanni Lorenzo Patarini (see note 70 above). Both were under thirty years of age.

78. See note 37 above.

79. This may be a reference to Louis Harmeville, who was born near Verdun about 1528, entered the Jesuits in Rome (1550), and died at Pont-à-Mousson on October 4, 1578.

80. Palmio was born in Parma in 1518, and became a Jesuit in 1547. He was rector of the community in Bologna at this time, and died there on April 23, 1585.

81. The rector in Florence was Louis Coudret, born in Savoy in 1523. He entered the Society in Rome (1546), and died in Paris on November 12, 1572.

82. This seems to be a reference to a member of the community known simply as Father Desiderio. He was a Frenchman, born about 1521, entered the Society in Rome (1550), and died in Florence on July 19, 1561.

83. The two priests in Gubbio were the rector, Alberto Ferrarese (see note 99 below), and Giovanni Agostino Riva, who was born in Padua about 1503. Riva became a Jesuit in 1552 and died in Loreto on August 17, 1563.

84. This theologian was Everard Mercurian, rector of the college in Perugia. He was born about 1515 at Marcourt, in Luxembourg, and entered the Society in Paris in 1548. He served as

rector in Perugia (1552–57), provincial of Flanders (1558–65), German assistant (1565–72), and general of the Society (1573–80). He died in Rome on August 1, 1580.

85. This was Jean Lenoir, a Frenchman, known among the Jesuits as Niger. He entered the Society as a priest in Rome in 1552, and died at Ferrara on February 17, 1555.

86. Martin Olave was also dean of the Roman College. He was born in Vitoria, Spain, about 1512, was ordained in 1544, and received his doctorate from Paris in the same year. He became a Jesuit in Rome (1552), and died there on August 17, 1556.

87. Jean Couvillon was a Frenchman, born at Lille in 1523. He entered the Society at Louvain (1544), received his doctorate at Gandía (1550), and after teaching many years at the Roman College, died in Rome on August 17, 1581.

88. Berze was a Lowlander, having been born in Goes, in Zeeland, in 1515. He studied at Louvain, served in the army of Charles V, then exchanged the soldier's uniform for the garb of a hermit at Montserrat. He left to go to Portugal and entered the service of the royal treasurer, and while at court he met Simão Rodrigues, who eventually led him through the Exercises and accepted him into the Society on April 20, 1546. Berze was ordained before the end of that year, and shortly afterwards was assigned to India where he imitated Francis Xavier, not only in apostolic zeal, but also in holiness.

89. Polanco had written three letters to Berze under the date of December 24, 1553, and since there were no ships going to the East at the time, the letters had not yet left Italy.

90. His family name was Mancini, but he was known as de Attino because he had been born in the small town of Atina near Frosinone. He entered the Society in Rome in 1552, pronounced his vows in November of that year, and was then sent to Sicily. He returned to Atina and his health did get better, but since he again

found consolation and joy in being with his family he chose that consolation over the spiritual consolation of being with Jesuits, and left the Society in 1554.

91. The only thing known about this Pompilio is that he was a Roman.

92. The letter speaks of "the following points," but since there is nothing in the letter indicating such points, Ignatius may have been referring to something that was enclosed with the instruction, like a questionnaire, pointing out the qualities that ought to be present in someone desiring to enter the Society.

93. Bartolomeo's family name is unknown, but he was called Romano after the city of his birth. He joined the Jesuits in 1553, probably in Rome, but then left the Society in March 1556.

94. Cogordan was born in Provence, France, about 1502, and was a priest when he entered the Society in Paris in 1541. In December 1550 he became treasurer of the Jesuit residence in Rome. He was back in Paris in 1560 and died there on March 21, 1582.

95. Claysson was born in Bruges, Belgium, on December 21, 1529, and entered the Jesuits in Paris on April 1, 1549. He taught theology in Rome (1562–64), and returned to Bruges and died there on November 17, 1601.

96. Claysson's letter may be found in *Litterae quadrimestres* (*MHSI*) 3:194–96. These letters were so called because superiors outside Italy and within Europe were required to write to the general every four months. The superiors of Italian houses were to write every month, and those in missionary lands were to write once a year.

97. Ignatius here uses the Greek, το πρεπον.

98. Though the Society enjoyed the favor of King Henry II, and several bishops, it found that the Sorbonne, the Parlement, and the

Bishop of Paris, Eustace du Bellay, were opposed to it. Neither the Parlement nor the Sorbonne would approve the Society, and as recently as December 1, 1554, the Sorbonne succeeded in getting the Parlement to issue an indictment against the Society, stating that it was a menace to the faith, a disturber of peace in the Church, and that it sought to put an end to the monastic life. In his quarterly letter Claysson mentions that the Bishop of Paris was still issuing threats and that they did not expect anything favorable to come from the Sorbonne's theological faculty. Thus Ignatius somewhat jovially refers to the Sorbonne's penchant for issuing censures.

99. Ferrarese's family name was Azzolini, but because he had been born in Ferrara about 1510, his Jesuit brethren referred to him as Ferrarese. He entered the Society in Rome in 1552, had been rector of the college at Gubbio, and when that institution closed in 1554, he went to Venice. He died in Ferrara in April 1558.

100. Adriaenssens was a native of Antwerp, having been born there in 1520. He became a Jesuit at Louvain in 1545, and after his ordination in Cologne (1548), spent several months (late 1548–March 1549) in Rome. Upon his return to his homeland he became rector at Louvain, and died there on October 18, 1580.

101. James Brodrick, S.J., in *The Progress of the Jesuits (1556–1579)* (New York: Longmans, Green, 1947) 90, refers to Adriaenssens as one "who belonged to the school of those whose principle is, We have a law and according to that law he ought to die," and quotes a portion from a letter that Laínez wrote to Adriaenssens: "I commend to your Reverence care for the health of Master Adrian Witte. He sadly needs your sympathy. If you hesitate as to extremes, I beg you to choose the extreme of indulgent charity rather than that of severe repression."

102. Adrian Witte was known in the Society as Candidus. He was born in Antwerp, about 1529, and joined the Jesuits in Paris in 1550. He studied in Rome and was ordained there in 1552. He was then sent to preach in Modena and by 1554 he was at Louvain. He died there in January 1558.

103. Bernard Olivier was a Belgian, born in Antoing in 1523. He went to Rome in 1546 and worked with a notary, and when he entered the Society in 1549 he had already been ordained. He became minister (1550) of the house where Ignatius lived, then rector of the Roman College (1551), and in the beginning of 1553 went to Sicily because of his health. He returned to Flanders toward the end of that year. In May 1556 Ignatius appointed him the first provincial of Lower Germany (and Flanders); he died three months later after visiting a Jesuit ill with the plague. Olivier caught the dread disease and died in Tournai on August 22, 1556.

104. See note 18 above. Ribadeneira was in Flanders negotiating the establishment of new houses of the Society.

105. See 1 Cor. 8:13, and Rom. 14:21.

106. Since his family name never occurs in Ignatius's correspondence, it is impossible to identify him further.

107. De Bonis was born in Guastalla, in Lombardy, in 1531, and entered the Society in August 1550 in Rome. He was ordained in Rome in 1560 and served as rector of several colleges and gained a reputation for being an eloquent preacher. He died in Naples on April 10, 1595.

108. Juan Marin was born in Valencia, probably in 1529, and was commonly known among his Jesuit brethren as Valentino. He entered the Society in his native city in 1553, and then came to Italy for his studies. He was ordained in Palermo in 1556 and unexpectedly died at Bivona on September 16 of that year.

109. Jerónimo Doménech was provincial in Sicily. See note 72 above.

110. The rector at Bivona was Eleuthère Dupont, known in the correspondence as Pontanus. He was born in Lille, France, on October 27, 1527, and became a Jesuit in Paris on April 6, 1550. He was ordained in Rome in September 1555, and was then appointed

rector of the community in Bivona, Sicily. He died in Brussels on
January 31, 1611.

111. Androzzi was born in 1524 at Montecchio, in Macerata,
and was a canon at Loreto when the Society established a house in
that city (1554). He came to know Laínez, made the Exercises under
his direction, and then entered the Society in Rome in November
1555. Shortly thereafter he went to work in the province of Emilia.
He died in Ferrara on August 27, 1575.

112. Ortensio was Fulvio Androzzi's brother. Ortensio was
born in 1528, and became a Jesuit in Rome in March 1556, and was
in Rome when Polanco was writing to Fulvio. Ortensio died in
Rome on January 24, 1589.

113. Curzio was the youngest of the three Androzzi brothers.
He was born in 1536, and entered the Society in Loreto in April
1556, and was a novice at the time this letter was written. Curzio
died in Brescia on June 13, 1584.

114. Giovanni Filippo Vito was Polanco's assistant. He was
born in Messina in 1531, and became a Jesuit in February 1551. He
came to Rome to study, and in April 1554 began working with
Polanco. He was ordained the following year, and died in Rome on
April 8, 1558.

INDEX OF SCRIPTURAL PASSAGES

INDEX OF PERSONS